ADULT ~~RELATIONSHIP~~ SHIP SKILLS

Build Trust and Deepen Connection with Your Partner

NIC SALUPPO, M.A.

Contents

Workbook   1

Gift   2

Part I
Foundational Content   **3**

Introduction   4

What It Means to Be an Adult
in a Relationship   16

Soft Skills vs. Hard Skills   26

Part II
The Skills   **28**

Relationship Skill #1
Seek Truth at All Costs   29

Relationship Skill #2
Know What Type of Discussion
You're Having   36

Relationship Skill #3
Build And Use Your Voice   40

Relationship Skill #4
Own Your Therapeutic Insights   50

Relationship Skill #5
The Four Steps of Making Up   54

Relationship Skill #6
Forgiveness Has Limits   62

Relationship Skill #7
Keep Your Word   70

Relationship Skill #8
Listen to Understand,
Not Just to Respond   82

Relationship Skill #9
Ask Clarifying Questions   92

Relationship Skill #10
Don't Immediately Blame Your Partner   104

Relationship Skill #11
Happy Relationships Require More
than Financial Provision   113

Relationship Skill #12
Less Talk, More Action   119

Relationship Skill #13
Be Playful and Have Fun   126

Summary   132

One Last Thing   137

Workbook   138

Get in Touch   139

More from this Author: 140
  ➢ *Communicate Your Feelings*
    (without starting a fight)

  ➢ *Learn to Love Yourself Again*

  ➢ *Outsmart Negative Thinking*

Workbook

The personal workbook companion is intended to help you process the content and ingrain the relationship skills found in this book. It's available on Amazon.

Gift

Get the PDF Gift at
www.nicsaluppo.com/gifts

The Relationship Skills Sheet is meant for people who have read the entire book. Without the book's context, the PDF won't make sense. But with the context of the book in mind, it will act as a quick reminder when you don't have time to consult the book. The Relationship Skills Sheet summarizes important skills found in this book and includes practical actions you can immediately implement. Keep it on your device, hang it on the refrigerator, or put it in another convenient spot.

PART I

Foundational Content

Introduction

Acting The Part vs. Being The Part

Showing up as an adult in relationships requires a level of self-mastery. Simply speaking the correct lines or doing the correct actions can be categorized as acting like an adult. But there's a difference between acting like an adult versus being an adult on the inside. The skills in this book will guide you toward the necessary internal transformation to be an adult in your relationship, not just act the part.

As you read this book, you'll undergo a deep transformation in addition to learning one-liners and techniques for interacting with your partner to make your relationship more trust-filled and connected. This book will make the difference between having a tough conversation with your partner because you know you're *supposed to* (because that's what you "should" do in healthy relationships, right?) and having the tough conversation from a place of *wanting to* because you know it brings you closer together and prevents relationship corrosion. This book can make the difference between acknowledging your role in relational difficulties because it's the fair thing to do or for the purpose of getting your partner to respect you to acknowledging your role because something in you believes in the value of owning your missteps. This book will make the difference between having to *overcome* your ego to have the hard conversation or take responsibility for harmful words and actions and having your ego actually encourage you in these ways of being.

This book isn't about applying superficial techniques, it's about an inner transformation that will make you *be* an adult in your relationship rather than settle for *acting* like an adult.

Many people say about themselves, "I don't feel like an adult." "Adult" isn't a feeling. Fear, anxiety, joy, sadness, and so on are feelings. Saying you don't feel like an adult means, "When I was young, I thought the adults around me were in control and had things figured out. I don't have a sense of having things figured out. I thought being an adult would mean my uncertainty would be gone, I would be more confident in myself and around other adults, and I would know what I'm doing." With uncertainty comes anxiety, and with anxiety comes the belief that you must not be an adult. It's a cyclical pattern because your belief that adults don't experience uncertainty (and therefore, you must not be one) fuels the anxiety, and the anxiety then fuels the belief. It's time to step out of that pattern.

Most of us weren't taught how to do relationships. You simply picked up how the adults around you related to themselves, one another, and you. Additionally, most of us witnessed interactions that could be considered outright toxic, such as yelling, name-calling, stomping off, and door-slamming, followed by acting like it never happened a few hours later or the next day.

As bad, but rarely considered toxic (it is, though), is witnessing no disagreements. "Let's not argue in front of the kids," many parents say. "It'll upset them." I've met many people, not only clients, who have told me their parents never argued. Arguing could upset the kids. However, kids must witness the resolution of disagreements. Not witnessing this will cause much more harm when they're adults and have no idea how to enter into disagreements for the purpose of coming up with mutually agreeable solutions. So, yes, a child may feel fear or anxiety when she sees her parents arguing. But if the arguing is done fairly—no name calling, no sarcasm, both people respectfully express what's on their mind, and both make a genuine attempt to own their mistakes and find mutually agreeable resolutions—the temporary anxiety felt by the child will be washed away with relief when she sees that the argument ultimately led to a happier connection between her parents. Plus, she'll have witnessed essential conflict resolution skills she'll apply in adulthood with her partner.

For most of us, we witnessed either toxic ways of arguing or no arguing, and both experiences left us clueless about handling conflicts and issues in our adult relationships. It's not your fault nobody taught you to handle relationships in healthy ways. You can't be held responsible for what you didn't know, but the responsibility becomes yours as soon as you know otherwise. With this book, you'll undo unworkable relationship patterns while developing new, healthy patters. As you take the concepts in, notice what feelings and insights arise within you.

Anatomy of an Interaction

If you're interested in improving your relationship skills, that probably means you're looking for more happiness, connection, and emotional stability with less arguing, disconnection, push-pull dynamics and ups and downs.

Take any interaction between two people, and you'll quickly see that what you observe as the external interaction consists of the internal dynamics of the two people being expressed. As examples, someone who has something to say but isn't saying it could be experiencing an internal dynamic of fear or anxiety. Someone who's dominating a conversation could be experiencing an internal dynamic of desperately wanting to be seen, heard, and validated.

While we may not be able to pinpoint what internal dynamic someone else is experiencing without asking them a slew of clarifying questions, we can all agree that internal states determine external interaction. When you're happy and relaxed, you interact differently than when you're angry and frustrated. When you're scared, you interact differently than when you're confident. The self-directive *I better do everything exactly right* will lead to a different interaction than the self-directive *I'm free to respectfully experiment in this relationship and then discuss both of our feelings about it.*

Understanding that internal emotions, thoughts, and beliefs are the drivers of your external interactions with your partner is vital because not much can happen in terms of transformation without such insight. With that in mind, know that many of the adult relationship skills described here focus on noticing what's occurring within yourself. By noticing what's happening inside yourself, you give yourself the power of choice around that issue. You can't change something you don't know exists. But if you know it exists, you can now act in the best way you see fit pertaining to that issue. Additionally, when you notice what's happening within yourself, you can communicate it to your partner.

To exemplify this, take a couple I worked with, Laura and Steve. Steve wanted Laura to tell him if something was bothering her about him, the relationship, or if she had a preference in general. Laura would freeze up any time they tried to discuss such matters, retreating deeply into herself. After examining Laura's past, it came out that her father was aggressive toward her and her brother. Her father would tell her he wanted her to share what was going on with her, then he would tell her that her feelings were all wrong when she shared. He got in physical altercations with her brother multiple times. He would forcefully tell her how to live her life.

Steve showed genuine interest in Laura and demonstrated the skills to have adult discussions. However, if she shared anything with Steve, Laura was certain she'd be met with aggression, hostility, shaming tactics, and invalidation. The internal trauma caused by her father affected her so much she couldn't express a preference (e.g., "I'd like chicken, not spaghetti"), ask for help ("Can you finish the laundry while I do the dishes?"), or say what she felt ("I feel upset about what you said earlier, and I'd like to talk about it").

Internal attitudes, emotions, and beliefs affect external interactions in big ways, like in the case of Laura and Steve, and in smaller ways, like with a passing mood or working too many hours without enough rest one week. And while Laura displayed withdrawal behaviors, it also applies on the other side of the spectrum with overtly aggressive behaviors. When someone displays aggressive, controlling behaviors, an internal emotion, attitude, or belief is behind it. There's no such thing as "He's just a jerk" or "She just can't communicate." Something inside the person always drives these behaviors.

The key to improving your relationship is for both partners to become aware of their internal processes. A self-aware partner can say things like, "I notice I want to be argumentative right now because I perceived your comment as an attack," or "I notice I want to withdraw and hide right now because your facial expression seemed like you were judging me." A mutually self-aware person would be grateful their partner is letting them know about their internal experience instead of keeping it to themselves. They might respond with something like, "What about what I said seemed like an attack?" or "Can I tell you why I made that face?"

The point of identifying what's happening within yourself is to open up discussion. Discussion leads to mutual understanding, a source of relational strength, trust, and connection. With that in mind, many of the relationship skills in this book will require you to pause and evaluate your internal self. This differs from believing your first interpretation of a situation and responding based on that initial interpretation. To do this successfully, you may have to slow down your interactions. Put aside the need to respond within a split second of your partner completing their sentence. Mutually agree to go slower with your discussions so you can both become aware of what's happening internally.

Is the Book Title Implying I'm a Child?

Looking back, isn't it interesting that most of us assumed adults knew how to do relationships well? Whatever our parents or caregivers did, we thought it was normal. If your parents screamed, swore, and slammed doors, you may not have questioned it. Your body certainly questioned it by going into fight, flight, or freeze mode, but your conscious mind may have thought, *This is just how life is.*

If your parents never talked with you or one another about their feelings and life experiences, you thought that was normal.

Sure, you had a sense of being alone because that's how anyone would be if they have no one to talk with about their feelings and life experiences. But with nothing to compare that to, you took it as normal.

If mom relied on you for emotional support, that was normal. If dad constantly criticized you, normal. If mom was controlled by dad, normal. If dad cowered to mom, constantly trying to please her, normal. The billions of neurons in your body took this in subconsciously, and it formed your worldviews and ways of relating. Essentially, infants and children are like sponges. They unconsciously take in the attitudes and emotions that are most strongly present and then formulate their beliefs about themselves, relationships, and the world.

Know that if your relationships haven't been working, there's not something terribly wrong or abnormal about you.

Truly.

The simple truth is that you developed certain beliefs about yourself, relationships, and the world as a *necessary* reaction to the life you found yourself in as a baby and young child. If you are willing to become aware of the internal dynamics that drive your ways of relating to your partner, your relationship will change. If you have an attitude of "this is just how I am," this book will be useless to you. But for those interested, learning to relate in healthy ways is possible. A week from now, you can see changes. A few months from now, you can see new, healthy patterns. A year from now, you can look back and realize that everything has changed for the better.

But My Parents Were Really Nice

If your family or caregivers were explosive or outrightly abusive, it'll be easy for you to see how your current unworkable relationship patterns were at one time a necessary response to the environment around you. For example, if your parents constantly fought, you may have learned to protect yourself by retreating to your room or going outside to not be a victim of the untethered anger flying about the home. As a result, you withdraw when conflict arises between you and your partner. Yet, you're reading this book because you know deep down that effective conflict is necessary for a thriving partnership. As another example, you may have learned to fight and shout to defend yourself. How else would you get any attention in a family that only gave attention to the angriest, loudest, and most disruptive members? As an adult, you might explode at your partner when a conversation would be perfectly effective. Deep down, you know there's a better way to relate than through explosions, which brought you to this book.

The above examples make it easy to see the link between early childhood development and your current relationship patterns. If you're sitting here saying, "But my parents were so nice," it could be more difficult to see the link.

Maybe you're going through difficult, unworkable relationship patterns but see no link to your upbringing because your parents were such good people. My personal work has been obvious because I would wake up every weekend to doors slamming and words like "Asshole!" being yelled across the house. It wasn't difficult for me to say, "Hm, maybe I didn't have the most effective models for doing relationships in healthy ways." Conversely, many of my clients say, "My parents were really great people. I have no issues with them." They'll then describe horror stories in their adult relationships. Things like marrying abusers, narcissists, addicts, or finding themselves as an abuser, narcissist, or addict. #WTFMate?

How does it happen that a person's parents were upright people and outstanding citizens, yet somehow they learned to do relationships in ways that create only craziness? In my experience, there are three primary reasons. Number one, given that your parents were so nice, they never taught you how to effectively use your voice and stand up for yourself. Therefore, you either completely bury your voice in relationships or use it like an atomic bomb, both equally destructive.

While your parents never teaching you to use your voice and stand up for yourself isn't outright abuse, it is definitively neglect (however, that's not to say it was done intentionally). Without an effective voice, the options become either A) holding back your voice and needs or B) becoming explosive. To send someone into adulthood without having taught them to navigate confrontations and difficult conversations in relationships (your voice is required to navigate these areas) is to have set that person up for failure unknowingly.

Know that this isn't to blame your parents or caregivers. Healing doesn't require hating them. You can still love and respect them while recognizing they didn't teach you this crucial relationship skill. I suspect if they knew the skill, they absolutely would have taught you. These issues are generational and not the fault of any single individual. They didn't have the awareness you have. Since you have the awareness, you now hold in your hands the opportunity to change the generational cycle. This is about acknowledging that a key relationship skill is missing; it's not about blaming the people who brought you up. I spent this entire paragraph saying this so you can still appreciate your parents while acknowledging what they couldn't teach you. Some people think they're committing a mortal sin if they think of their parents in any way other than perfect. To acknowledge what was done well and what was missing in raising you is the mindset of an adult. As an adult, you can choose who you want to be or don't want to be. Identifying skills your parents didn't impart to you is not a betrayal. I would see it as more of a betrayal if my children didn't think for themselves as adults. If my children won't make their own way in life and are unconsciously attached to pleasing me when they're adults, then I have failed as a parent. As adults, I want them to follow the path of their deepest self without considering whether it would please me.

Number two, children with very nice parents had a sense of only being able to talk about nice things. If something happened that deeply affected you, you may have had a sense of needing to dull down the impact it had on you for your parents. On a 1-10 scale, the event was an eight, deeply affecting you, but you unconsciously wanted to protect your nice parents from your pain, so you described the incident as if it were a two or three. Or maybe you didn't tell them at all, choosing to bear it by yourself.

If you learned you must protect people from your big feelings, there's a chance your partner doesn't know the whole story of YOU. If they know little of your story and what makes you tick, then your relationship will suffer from superficiality. To have a sense of being loved deeply, we must risk being known deeply. As adults, vulnerability is necessary to have a sense of being loved by someone. Without it, you can never have a sense of someone loving you to your core because you haven't revealed your core to them. Not sharing who you are provides risk mitigation in that there's no chance of experiencing rejection. Without a strong sense of self, rejection is interpreted as annihilation, final, and unbearable. Having developed a sense of self, risking vulnerability becomes an exciting, curious part of relationships.

Number three, nice people are often unfeeling people. I've worked with client populations who, on one end of the spectrum, had explosive, abusive parents and, on the other end, parents who expressed no feelings whatsoever, instead keeping everything on the intellectual level. I truthfully cannot say which is more harmful to a developing child. With an explosive parent, at least the child gets to see that anger is an emotion that exists. That child will then hide their anger out of fear of either causing damage *by* expressing it or being hurt by someone else *for* expressing it or that child will pick up on the modeling and express anger explosively.

With a parent who expresses no feelings, the child learns they're not okay at the core of who they are because, whether expressed or not, the child experiences feelings. Since every human experiences emotion, the underlying, unconscious message given to the child by a parent who never expresses or deals with their own emotions is: Your emotions are not okay. They are unacceptable. For the child, the message becomes: I am not okay. I am unacceptable. Such children are more likely to repress rather than suppress. Repression is unknowingly holding your emotions down, while suppression is knowingly holding them down. With suppression, you can choose in any situation. With repression, an unconscious choice was made long ago.

Your feelings are locked in a scary room down in the basement, and you've forgotten the room exists.

In this section, I spoke to people who may have experienced their parents as nice people. I thought that group could use more information to decide if this book is for them. This book is for anybody who realizes their relationship skills aren't working for them. Sometimes, it will help to know where your dysfunctional ways of relating came from. In other instances, you may not need to know where they came from; it will be enough to simply recognize that what you're doing isn't working and replace it with a new relationship skill.

What It Means to Be an Adult in a Relationship

What does it mean to be an adult in relationships? It means replacing habitual, conditioned patterns of relating with consciously chosen ways of relating. I know no one who tells a potential partner, "Just so you know, if you're ever upset or angry with me, I'm going to emotionally curl up inside myself and choose not to speak or communicate. A few hours later or the next day, I'll act like nothing ever happened. Just a heads up." When these relational patterns happen, they're habitual, not consciously chosen. Likewise, I know no one who says, "Hey, since we've been together a few weeks, I think now is a good time to tell you that if I'm ever upset or angry with you, I'm going to scream at you, call you names, and throw anything I can get my hands on. Here, I bought you this helmet so you can wear it when I inevitably go into a blind fit at some point in the next few months."

Don't be hard on yourself about this. Nobody goes into a relationship consciously enacting childlike behaviors. Yet, they enact such behaviors, and that's because strong neural networks hold together the defense mechanisms programmed into us at a young age. A neural network works like an automated program. Consider how if you don't buckle up when you turn your car on, it will ding at you. "Hey! Ding-ding-ding—your seatbelt isn't on." Also, when you look at your phone, the time is automatically updated minute to minute with no effort from you. An automated program guides your emotional reaction when you perceive someone to be angry, upset, withholding, overbearing, smothering, etc. *Ding-ding-ding—something's wrong here!*

How you respond to your partner is often determined by an automatic emotional reaction. Unconscious, programmed thoughts might sound like *I'm angry, so that means I'll use sarcasm*, or *I'm scared, so that means I'll sit and nod my head with the hope that the more agreeable I am, the sooner this interaction will be over.* We don't choose to behave in childlike ways, but our neural networks automatically go into action, and we behave in ways we would never want to choose.

So, back to the question: What does it mean to be an adult in relationships? It means becoming aware of your automated programs, processing the emotions associated with them, then consciously choosing a healthy response. It's helpful to view this as three steps:

1.   Become aware of your automated programs.

2.   Process the emotions associated with your automated programs.

3.   Consciously choose a healthy response.

There's a significant difference between child and adult consciousness, which involves where awareness lies. For a child, everything is focused on the outer world. The child must reach outside of herself with her lips for her mother's nipple or bottle. When uncomfortable from soiling himself, he must vocalize outwardly so a caregiver will clean up his mess and make the discomfort go away. Young children rely on someone else to cook and place food on the table for them. When emotionally upset, children rely on external soothing, such as someone caressing their hair or rubbing their back. A young child's consciousness is almost exclusively outward, so much so they can't tell when they must go to the bathroom. They'll go anywhere, anytime. It makes no difference to them whether they poop their pants in the car, at a party, at church, or in the comfort of their own home. An infant has no understanding that he's peeing right into the face of the person changing his diaper.

Infants and young children have no concept of existing as individuals and other people existing as separate individuals. There's not much understanding that their desires are not the same as the desires of others. Others are an extension of themselves. The child wants others to be controlled by the thoughts and wishes of his mind. He hasn't yet developed the ability to bring his awareness inside and engage in self-reflection. *Self-reflection* is the determining variable that shifts a person's life from child consciousness to adult consciousness.

The term self-reflection innately indicates having a sense of self. Having a sense of self then indicates a sense of being aware that others are separate. If this weren't the case, there would be no need for a sense of "self." We would all go through life with a pure sense of beingness. Yet, others exist. Sometimes others treat us well, and sometimes they treat us poorly or even abuse us.

If a child's developmental needs for affection, emotional warmth, acceptance, positive mirroring, discipline without rejection of them as a person, and food are met, they'll be able to accurately self-reflect in adulthood. Accurate self-reflection leads to effective and healthy navigation of adult relationships. How frustrating it is to be in a relationship with someone who can't self-reflect accurately. They might apologize when there's nothing to apologize for, or place blame on you when they're the one who needs to take responsibility. They might see themselves as unworthy of mutual participation in the relationship (e.g., both of our needs and wants are equally important), or they might rationalize away their responsibilities and commitments. When a person's developmental needs go unmet, they'll show up in relationships in childlike ways. But if you're aware this is happening, you can work through it, showing up in healthier ways.

In my own life, I learned to repress my emotions. As a two-year-old, I was locked out of the house for expressing anger, a tremendous psychological trauma. I quickly learned to be quiet and not make any noise lest I be shut out. It was instinctually a matter of survival since, at two years old, I was as good as dead if I were shut out and left outside to fend for myself. I required a dedication to therapy, workshops, reading, journaling, and self-awareness to break my cycle of repression. Now, I welcome all of my emotions because I know holding them down only leads to bigger problems. *All* emotions express themselves one way or another, whether through relational dynamics, psychological issues, or medical manifestations. Sidenote: If you're in a place where you can't adequately express your emotions, such as work or a social function, it's okay to come back to it when you have privacy. Just don't forget to come back to it, otherwise, the emotion will stew in the basement of your psyche and cause more problems later.

Children naturally express whatever emotion arises in them, calming down once the feelings have been expressed. If a child isn't able to freely express themselves during the infant and toddler years, they'll become either repressed or explosive in the years of later childhood, adolescents, and adulthood. A repressed person expresses their emotions unconsciously, and this often looks like making agreements and not following through (a passive-aggressive way of saying "no"), developing stress-related medical conditions, or developing mental health challenges. Emotions will express themselves consciously or unconsciously—there's absolutely no stopping them. Repression causes psychological and physiological stress, it's just that you're unaware of it. You might even think it's normal to constantly have a vague sense you're carrying a 200-pound rock on your back. If life seems constantly heavy, it's a sign of repression, which is unconscious. Once you're aware of it, it's not repression, it becomes suppression. Suppression is the conscious choice to hold down emotion. Once you express your emotions, old and new, you're neither repressed nor suppressed—you're open and in flux. Humans are similar to stale water because it gets icky fast. A spring gives off clean water because it moves up through the ground, filtering out anything toxic, and then expresses itself as it leaves the ground. A spring is always in flux. When we don't express our emotions and deal with the pains of life, we become emotionally and psychologically stale. This subject was the focus of many of my previous books, including *Learn to Love Yourself Again* and *Trauma: Curative Concepts*. Additionally, other great resources on this subject include *When the Body Says No* by Gabor Mate and *Healing Trauma* by Peter Levine.

An explosive person expresses their emotions <u>at</u> people. They're able to do this because they've projected the blame of not having their needs met during their infant and toddler years onto the present people in their lives. The explosive person's caregivers are responsible for not meeting his needs as a child, and what he's screaming and yelling about all the time is the lack of his needs having been met back then. Show me a boss who treats his employees like crap, and I'll show you a person whose developmental needs weren't met. Show me a person who can never take self-ownership over wrongdoing, and I'll show you a person whose developmental needs weren't met. Everyone in the world, if they don't meet his needs perfectly, will be unconsciously put in the same category as his parents, who didn't meet the needs of his younger years. To clarify, when I say the parents didn't meet the responsibility of meeting this person's developmental needs, this isn't to assign blame. Dysfunctional families are generationally created, and nobody who participates knows it. If they knew it, they wouldn't participate. It happens automatically until someone in the family line is exposed to (and open to) the concept of emotional health and healing.

In being locked out of the house for expressing anger, I went down the path of repression. I was a quiet, awkward, and agreeable child. I was so repressed that when offered pizza at a friend's birthday party, I said, "No, thank you," but I was starving. I wanted that pizza badly. To be so repressed that you can't even express the most basic need of hunger is to be repressed at the most severe level. Some years later, the athletic director at school violently grabbed me by the throat. If you're following my pattern of repression, you can probably guess I told nobody. I began developing voice symptoms over the next few years. Eventually, my life became so problematic and miserable that I couldn't ignore it any longer. My voice had stopped functioning properly, and I was fantasizing about suicide daily. This was a do-or-die point. I had to act because if I got any worse, I likely would have ended my life. That's how bad it had to get for me to seek psychological help. For me to break out of my repression took being on the brink of self-imposed death. Consider for yourself: If you lean more toward explosiveness in your relationship, how much will it take for you to get support in expressing yourself in healthy, nondestructive ways? Or if you lean more toward repression, suppression, and withdrawal, how much will it take to begin finding ways to express who you are to your partner? Really, how much more will it take to decide that now is the time to work on these areas? Let the pain you've experienced in life up to this point be enough. Let the ongoing issues you've had, whether personal or relational, be enough. Don't wait until a separation, mental health issue, or other crisis scenario to take the steps of healing and growth. For me, life tried to wake me up by tickling me with a feather. I ignored that, so it tapped me on the shoulder. I ignored that, so it grabbed me by the arms and shook me. I ignored that, so life sent Casey Jones to hit me in the face with a hockey stick, and there was no way to ignore that. Let us be attentive to the gentle ways life tries to get our attention.

Bringing it back to the concept of self-reflection, if your developmental needs of affection, emotional warmth, acceptance, positive mirroring, discipline without rejection, and food weren't met adequately, then you'll either never develop the ability to self-reflect, or you'll be able to self-reflect, but what you see will be twisted and not reflect reality.

I was able to self-reflect, but everything I came up with was twisted. For example, "I'm angry and hurt you didn't keep our plans (accurate). Maybe if I were good enough, you would have kept them (inaccurate)." Or "I'm deeply disturbed about the athletic director grabbing me by the throat (accurate). It was somehow probably my fault (inaccurate)." You can see how accurate sensibilities become twisted, making it difficult to live in reality.

Another example of twisted self-reflection is constantly thinking it's your responsibility to fix the relational riffs of other people. A client and his spouse formed a blended family. This client's wife was having relational difficulties with her adult son. The son lived in another state and chose not to reach out on Mother's Day. This client took it upon himself to contact the son and reproach him for not contacting his mother on Mother's Day.

#Whoopsie
#LetThemFigureOutTheirRelationship
#TheyAreBothAdults

This client forgot that the relational riffs of other adults aren't his responsibility.

Why is it so hard to remember it isn't your job to solve everybody else's arguments and relationship problems? It has to do with believing your emotional needs never mattered, but someone else's needs did matter, like an adult's or sibling's. As an adult, when other people aren't getting along, your automated programming turns on, firing off the neural networks. Suddenly, before you know what even hit you, you're trying to fix everything. We all intuitively know the ending of the story about my client: His meddling made it worse. He felt worse and his stepson felt worse and was now angry at both him and his mom.

Concerning adults, deal only with the people and interactions that are about you directly. Let other adults navigate their issues with one another in their own ways. It might feel uncomfortable but consider my client once again. Automated programming develops in areas that involve safety and self-protection. As a child, the environment isn't safe if people are arguing. If the people who are supposed to protect you are fighting, then nobody might be left to protect you. But in the example with my client, was he in danger? His conditioning was telling him he was, and that's why his emotions drove him to intervene between his wife and stepson. But was he actually in danger? With his stepson in another state and he and his wife comfortably at home, there was no danger to be found. Your alert system might go off, and you'll interpret it as danger. *Ding-ding-ding!* Before you insert yourself in relationship issues involving other adults, first ask yourself if danger is present. If you're asked to mediate, do it if you want to and don't do it if you don't want to. You're not obligated. As soon as you become stressed in the mediation process, stop. Say, "I'm not comfortable doing this any longer. I suggest the two of you seek a professional counselor to help you work this out." If you have children, you're responsible for helping them work through their issues. With two adults, that's not on you. As a child, you took it on unknowingly. Today, you can choose to stop doing that.

We went over three ways self-reflection becomes twisted. In the example of me getting locked out of the house, I came to see things as my fault that weren't. In the example of an explosively angry person, we saw how they blame essentially everyone for their needs not being met during their early years. And in the example of my client getting involved in issues between his stepson and spouse, we saw how he thought it was his responsibility to fix the relationship issues of other adults.

To activate adult relationship skills, you must first recognize that programming from a young age, sometimes as young as infanthood or the toddler years, is driving your current ways of relating. Once you realize this, you can process the young

24

feelings without having them insert themselves into your relationship. To not project your young feelings onto your partner is a sign of true care and love for your partner. After processing those feelings when they come up, you can choose a new relationship pattern. Processing your emotions means allowing them to flow through you. Don't block them or stop them. They operate much like waves. An emotion will arise, gaining momentum. It will reach its peak, crash, and then lose intensity from there. Ride the full wave without fighting it, then engage in conversation to sort things out with your partner. If you need to step away intermittently to ride a wave during conversation, that's okay.

Soft Skills vs. Hard Skills

Regarding skill, there are three primary states:

1. Lack of Skill

2. Hard Skill

3. Soft Skill

Take the skill of sprinting in track and field, for example. If you've never learned to sprint with proper form, it'll show. Your arms will move side to side, your legs will push off laterally instead of straight ahead, causing you to look like you're running in a zigzag, your toes will be pointed like a ballerina's, you'll reach for more distance with your feet, you'll grit your teeth and scrunch up your face, and you'll swing your arms at the elbow joint instead of the shoulder joint.

Then a trainer comes along and says, "Here's how you move your arms using the shoulder joint instead of bending and flexing the elbow. Also, here's how you cycle your legs instead of reaching with them." As you practice these new concepts, it'll show you've gained knowledge and put it into action. Hard skills are developing, but when you practice sprinting with your new form, it still looks mechanical, robotic.

You continue practicing daily for months. Eventually, moving your arms at the shoulder joint and cycling your legs become natural. You do it with no thought. You look smooth and graceful. You make it your own. Soft skills have developed.

Let's take this concept and apply it to relationships. Using the example of apologizing, there are three levels. First, no apology, showing a complete lack of skill. Second, the right words are spoken, "I'm sorry," but the voice tone sounds mechanical or forced, showing a hard skill. There may not be a true understanding of the psycho-emotional dynamics involved in the hurtful interaction. Third, the words "I'm sorry" are spoken with your tone and facial expressions, also communicating sorrow. You understand the damage caused to the other person. There's a naturalness to it, indicating sincerity and showing the blossoming of a soft skill.

Some skills you'll learn in this book will be hard skills, e.g., say this, not that, or do this, not that. However, many will be soft skills. Relationally speaking, a soft skill involves working with your internal psycho-emotional states of being, as what you are on the inside determines the quality and depth of relationship with your partner on the outside. Developing soft skills will distinguish between saying you're sorry in a forced way and saying it so your partner subconsciously knows you mean it and will therefore open their heart back up to you. Hard skills are about the right words and actions, while soft skills are about your deepest self aligning with your words and actions.

As you go through this book, distinguish whether the particular skill you're learning requires something of you internally (soft skill) or can be effective when applied through speech or outward action alone (hard skill).

PART II

The Skills

Relationship Skill #1
Seek Truth at All Costs

Instead of trying to win, seek truth at all costs.

Would you rather A) be given kudos and have your partner say you were right while missing a key piece of information that proves you weren't right, or B) have all the information and acknowledge that you were wrong in service of truth and reality prevailing?

One way we bring our child selves into a partnership is by insisting on winning and being right. If you had siblings, especially older ones, you may have learned it sucks to be last, and the winner is always best. Maybe a parent fostered competition and enacted shaming tactics when mistakes were made. In school, this conditioning was reinforced with all the kids wanting to be the best at something and heartlessly, mercilessly putting down those who aren't at their level with some particular skillset or ability. If you don't know how to pronounce a word when reading out loud, you might get laughed at. You might get made fun of if you're not a very athletic child. As adults, there are unspoken judgments that people in certain career fields are more deserving of respect than those in other fields, and the fight to socially achieve a place at the top amongst your peers continues in a more passive-aggressive manner. Because of familial and societal conditioning, we've come to believe being wrong, ever, and not always being right or being the best, is unacceptable.

As a therapist, I've heard the statement, "My partner has a really hard time admitting when they're wrong and apologizing," too many times to count. It's a rampant problem in relationships. Consider that in our society of constantly striving for success and proving you're worthy of standing above the rest, you are celebrated for coming out on top and shamed for losing. But when you're married, there's no audience. Nobody's going to cheer you on for silencing your partner when you're clearly in the wrong—that's between the two of you with no social reward. There could be negative consequences because your partner will likely pull away.

For many, this is an exceedingly difficult topic. Giving up the need to be right can be like taking a spear to the heart because we were taught to win at all costs and that if you don't win, well, you're nothing but a loser. In intimate relationships, people respect someone who can acknowledge when they're wrong and don't respect a win-at-all-costs attitude. Couples will argue with one another to the death (emotionally speaking) to avoid admitting where they were wrong. Some get very good at talking their way out of taking responsibility.

There are partners who take pride in their ability to win arguments by talking their partner into seeing things differently. Clients often say of their partner, "He's just so smart. He always turns it back around on me." Two things about that: First, people who constantly turn things back around on the other person are usually emotionally crippled. Intellectually, they're firing on all cylinders but have little capacity to sit with uncomfortable emotions. Second, turning things around only works on someone who thinks it's their duty to answer every question they're asked or respond to every comment the other person makes about them. Let's look more closely at these two concepts.

First, someone who is emotionally crippled has to turn every issue back around on you. As a child, a parent or caregiver sliced into this person so deeply that they never emotionally recovered. Instead, they got really good at relying on their intellect to maneuver their way out of emotional situations. Having been deeply shamed, possibly even shunned, for showing normal human emotions like fear or sadness, they made an unconscious agreement within themselves to never again show what they perceive as weak emotions. This got them through childhood successfully, but it's killing their relationships in adulthood. Who can stand being with someone who never takes responsibility for their wrongdoings?

"Hey, I really didn't like when you called me an idiot."

- "Well, maybe if you would actually think before you act, I wouldn't call you that."
- "After what you did, you have the nerve to bring up something so little?"
- "Why do you have to be so sensitive?"

Having a statement like, "I didn't like when you called me an idiot," turned back around onto you only works if you think you're obliged to answer every question or statement thrown your way.

- "What do you mean I don't think before I act?"
- "I know, what I did was way worse. I am really sorry for what I did."
- *I guess he's right. I have really thin skin. Maybe if I didn't have such thin skin, it wouldn't bother me so much. I guess I am too sensitive.*

31

When someone attempts to turn something around on you, you're not obligated to answer any of their questions or respond to any of their statements. Stay on track. You can say, "Listen, I'm telling you I don't like it. Even if it's true that I didn't think before I acted, you saying that is still unacceptable." Or "You're right, I have faults, too. I'm willing to own those and talk about them with you. But first, I want to address this issue of you calling me an idiot. Me having done something wrong doesn't make it okay to call me that name." Or "You call it sensitive, but I think name-calling is unacceptable, period. Whether you think it's sensitive or not, you calling me that isn't acceptable to me, period."

Sometimes, someone who tries turning something around on you will make a statement with a hint of truth. To prevent them from turning it around on you, follow two steps:

1. Acknowledge the hint of truth. (Go back and see how this was done in the example responses above.) Acknowledging neutralizes but defending or fighting fuels the flame.

2. Stick to your subject matter. You have a point you want to make, that being called a name isn't acceptable, so stick to it. Don't get pulled off track by their questions and comments. Insist that you'll address their issue after your issue is addressed.

If the statement has no grain of truth in it whatsoever, you can say, "Even if that were true, it's still not okay for you to call me an idiot."

If you find yourself as the one turning things around on your partner when they bring a reasonable issue to you, you'll have to work on building your emotional capacity. You'll need to do three things:

1. Think of the relationship as its own entity.

2. Become aware of your emotions.

3. Respond as a partner instead of as an individual.

With relationships, there's you, there's your partner, and there's the relationship. You exist as your own individual, and so does your partner. How you interact with one another creates the invisible entity of the relationship. It's a living, breathing, evolving, dynamic entity, but you can't see it in the same way you can see a physical structure. Every time a conversation that needs to happen is forgone, the relationship suffers a little. When the issue is finally discussed and addressed, the relationship regenerates. You might use your intellect to turn your partner away from confronting you about something, but the relationship diminishes. Your partner may give up on the issue because they know they can't verbally outmaneuver you. But how are they feeling emotionally about you and the relationship? There's a definitive loss of connection. If you're more verbally adept than your partner regarding debates and arguments, don't abuse that. Adopt a *Strength with Honor and Integrity* mindset. Proactively point out your weaknesses and the accurate observations your partner is making. If you never allow yourself to be receptive to your partner's reasonable concerns, the relationship will attenuate more and more. While you may have been able to talk your way out of apologizing or making your wrongs right over a period of years, the heart and soul of the relationship itself will be dead. With the aforementioned in mind, can you see how what you viewed as defending yourself is taking a toll on the relationship?

To change this pattern, you'll have to become aware of your emotions. When your partner comes to you with a reasonable concern, notice what's in the space between hearing their concern and your attempt to talk your way out of it. If you observed anger is in that space, you didn't look deeply enough. When you go deeper, you'll discover fear, sadness, and shame. Such emotions can be so painful that we cover them up with anger to avoid knowing they're there. If you don't let yourself feel these emotions, you're going to constantly react by being defensive and aggressive and using your intellect to get your partner to leave you alone.

As an extreme example, let's look at cheating. I've worked with cases where a partner was caught cheating, denied it, caught again, and then left the current relationship for the person they cheated with. Whether someone wants to leave a partnership is their decision, but why the denial? Why say they weren't cheating when it's apparent they were? The answer: fear, sadness, and shame. These feelings are so painful that a person will often fight to the death to avoid them. As an alternative, you can allow yourself to take an hour to break down emotionally, feel the fullness of the fear, sadness, and shame, then come back to your partner for an honest discussion. To break the cycle, you'll have to become aware of the emotions you're defending yourself from feeling. When you're capable of feeling painful feelings, you can pursue honest discussion because there aren't any feelings to avoid.

Last, respond as a partner and not as an individual. The individual instinct is to fight, win, convince, succeed, and prevail. Except, prevailing by denying a reasonable conversation with your partner slowly kills the lifeblood and vitality of the relationship. Instead, ask, *What response would be best for the soul of the relationship, not just me as an individual?*

Truly, it takes courage to feel the pain of having committed wrongdoing and acknowledge it. Doing so is a conscious decision to feel pain. Navy SEALs make a decision to feel pain when they enter training, particularly so during Hell Week. Similarly, to break the cycle of talking your way out of apologies and ownership for hurtful actions, you must feel the emotional pain. When you say the words, "What I did was wrong, and I'm sorry," how do you feel on the inside? Notice the feelings and embrace them like a Navy SEAL embraces the freezing cold water.

As a final note, I'm not a proponent of apologizing to keep the peace. If you did nothing wrong, don't apologize. This section has been specifically for those who know they are in the wrong but cannot bring themselves to take ownership.

Seeking truth at all costs is countercultural. It requires a willingness to embrace the consequences and implications of whatever the truth may be, even if it's contrary to you looking like a good person. To be certain, there can be immense pain in seeking truth rather than a personal victory over your partner. However, the pain of seeking truth is nothing compared to the drawn-out pain of trust slowly eroding away. Additionally, the trust and respect you'll gain from your partner when you seek truth above all far outweighs the initial emotional pain of siding with reality over personal defense.

Relationship Skill #2
Know What Type of Discussion You're Having

Instead of giving knee-jerk responses, first determine the type of discussion you're having.

In your relationship, you'll engage in three primary types of discussions: fun, expressive, and problem-solving.

I worked with a couple, James and Elise, who had trouble getting on the same page. James explained he was trying to sort out a big decision in his life, a career change, that would affect his wife, but his wife would offer no feedback or opinions on the matter. "I bring up this subject and tell her what I'm thinking," James said, "but she just nods and has nothing to say."

"I'm just trying to be a listening ear for you," Elise responded.

"I don't need a listening ear," James explained, "I need to problem-solve the next steps. I want insight, opinions, and ideas."

"Well, I don't want to tell you what to do. It's your career," Elise said.

James turned to me and said, "This is how our conversations go."

"Elise," I asked, "what kind of conversation do you think James is wanting?"

"Well, I don't know, but I just do my best to listen," Elise said.

"Is that what he wants?"

"Everyone wants to be listened to," she said.

I looked back to James, and he said to Elise, "I want you to hear what I'm saying, of course, but I don't have a sense of needing to vent. I'm not emoting out loud or just getting it off my chest. There's a practical issue that needs to be solved, and it affects you, too, so I want your input."

As you can see, James was engaging in a problem-solving conversation, but Elise was responding as if it was an expressive conversation. For any human, fun, expression, and problem-solving are necessary to live a whole and satisfying life. That's not to say it's your partner's responsibility to fulfill all your needs for fun, expression, and problem-solving. It's simply impossible for one human to do that for you. That's why we have communities, associates, acquaintances, friends, family, therapists, twelve-step groups, therapy groups, workshops, retreats, and so on.

Sometimes, your partner has a need you can't fill. They may have a serious, ongoing issue with a parent, and you're just not up for hearing about it today. If you know that your partner's current need is to emotionally express or problem-solve about their relationship with that parent, you can say, "I'm hearing you that you need to get this out right now, but I just don't have the capacity today." You might go on to say, "It takes a lot out of me to hear about this so often. I think it takes a lot out of me because I try hard to be supportive and engaged. I can handle talking about it twice per week, but not more than that." Your statement makes it clear that you see your partner's need. It makes it clear that you're putting in effort when discussing this topic. It's not that you don't give a sh*t. You understand exactly what they need, but you can't fulfill that need every single time. It will serve your partner better to have a complete support system around the issue and not just one person. For example, they can talk with you twice per week, a therapist once per week, a friend once per week, another friend once per week, and a support group every other week. This will serve their situation infinitely better than relying solely on one person for support.

If Elise understood what James needed, she could have asked herself if it was something she was up for discussing. If it was, then she could have given her opinions and ideas. "I feel scared about you doing a career change because there's no guarantee it'll work out," she might've said. Or she might've said, "I think your friends might have better insights than me, but I'm supportive of whatever you choose. I support you pursuing this." These answers express an understanding of what James wanted out of the conversation while still engaging the way she saw fit.

Understanding what type of conversation you or your partner want isn't about always meeting their need every time. It's about determining for yourself what you can offer and then expressing your understanding of their need. Usually, partners are happy to meet whatever need is being asked, within reason. For example, regularly listening to your partner emotionally express for 20 minutes is reasonable, but an hour or two is draining. This isn't to say never have long conversations where one person is expressing themselves, but if it's happening often, the one doing all the listening could be fatigued.

To get more specific in defining the three types of conversations, consider these descriptions:

A **Problem-Solving Conversation** is geared toward thinking about potential solutions for a situation in which the next step is not yet determined. This could range from deciding what's for dinner to discussing moving to a different state to how to handle a family member if they react negatively to a joint decision you and your partner have made.

The purpose of an **Expressive Conversation** is to express feelings for the purpose of unloading them. It's not about determining a course of action. This could range from something as simple as a one-sentence expression to five or 10 minutes of emotions about a particular experience or person.

A **Fun Conversation** is for pleasure alone. If you're working hard to listen or problem-solve, it's probably taking something out of you. Fun conversations can be about what's happening at this moment, being playful with one another, a funny memory, anecdotes, flirtation, sharing experiences from before you knew one another, and what happened today. Ensure fun conversations have a fairly equal exchange of speaking and listening. If you're someone who says little, be cognizant of sharing more. If you're someone who usually does 95% of the talking, be aware of cutting that in half so your partner can also have a sense of sharing themselves and being heard.

Asking yourself what kind of conversation you're engaged in will help you and your partner remain on the same page.

Relationship Skill #3
Build And Use Your Voice

Instead of making yourself small, build up your voice and use it.

I've wanted to write about this subject for some time now, as it's, unfortunately, a common issue. I've worked with many people, most of them women, who were never taught to stand up for themselves and make their own decisions. This issue affects more women than men due to cultural factors. Often, even if a man is raised in an environment where he's abused or neglected, cultural images of what it means to be a man motivate him to learn to use his voice, at least a little. The messages men get are to get out there, push through, and get it done . . . no matter what. Such a man might have a sense of constantly lugging a half-ton weight on his back, but he's moving forward and making progress. If he thinks speaking up for himself is what "a real man" does, he'll make an effort.

Women who aren't taught to use their voices, stand up for themselves, and make their own decisions, especially in the face of opposition, don't have as many cultural images to emulate. Therefore, they often stay stuck in this space, never realizing it's even an option to take up for themselves and determine their own path.

With the women I've worked with, the story is always some version of their parents never teaching them to use their voice and make their own decisions. There was always a sense of their path being laid out for them, usually by their fathers, and they were expected to follow that path. If she didn't follow the path her father wanted, she would be met with hostility. It seems the men who raised these daughters thought it was their duty to tell them *what to do* rather than teaching them *how to decide* what to do for themselves. Such daughters had no sense they could explore options in life and choose for themselves. Their fathers were so intent on sending them down a particular life path that these daughters didn't realize other options even existed. Note that it's not always the father—it's whichever parent or caregiver behaved in the most aggressively controlling manner.

Being raised in a way that didn't teach you how to use your voice, stand up for yourself, and trek your own path through life is neglect at best. When I say this to a woman early in working together, they'll often stare back blankly as if the idea that it was the duty of their parents to teach them how to make decisions (and not which decisions to make) was stated in a foreign language.

The men with difficulty using their voice respond in a knowing way when their parents not teaching them to use it is mentioned. Because of the cultural images all around, from super-hero movies to influencers on YouTube and Instagram, they seem to know that having a voice is a possibility even if they haven't yet developed it.

The issue that comes up next is shared across genders. It's how to use your voice without causing more drama. One client would work hard at his job all week and look forward to relaxing by watching football on Sundays. His wife, however, wanted to constantly work. She worked all week and on the weekends. The home and financial needs were being met, yet her line of thinking was that she doesn't take breaks, so neither should he.

There's an easy solution to this problem, and that would be for him to say, "You don't have to take a break, but I'm going to give myself time to relax." But if he said this, how would she respond? Regarding his partnership, he hadn't developed his voice.

In another case, a woman didn't know how to maintain her values when her husband had different values. She often gave in to her husband's values, leaving her with a sense of betraying herself. If she stood her ground, what would happen? When a man raises his daughter to do what he says and live how he wishes, he thinks he's imparting his way of life to her. Think again. What he's actually doing is programming her not think for herself and to do whatever the next significant man in her life wants. This is usually a boyfriend or husband, but it could also be a boss, therapist, or clergy member. Some therapists will gladly continue telling her what to do. If she works with a wise therapist, that therapist will teach her to think for herself and use her voice.

Here we are at this juncture of wanting to use your voice but not wanting more drama. What to do?

There's unfortunate news, and there's also fortunate news. The unfortunate news is that if you've spent your life not using your voice, you probably have a few current friendships and/or relationships based on an unconscious agreement of you obliging whatever the other person wants. To change such patterns, you will have to rock the boat. Yes, waves will be made. The fortunate news is that if the other person is doing their own inner healing work, they'll be happy for you and want to work with you as you develop your voice. If they're not doing their inner work, they'll be angry, resentful, and maybe attempt to be even

42

more overtly controlling when you make this change because they want to bring you back to how things used to be (i.e., you conceding to what they want). Why's that good news? It will tell you where the people in your life stand, especially your partner.

Is your partner happy for you or are they pissed that you won't bend like a noodle anymore? The wife of a friend has had difficulty stating her wishes for many years. My friend tells me that recently, she asked him if he would look for and grab all the towels when doing the laundry. Apparently, he'd done a load of towels but left a few in a corner behind the door. My friend explained that he gladly responded, "Yes, absolutely." He was happy to see his wife using her voice for the first time in their relationship. He said they were having a conversation a couple weeks later and he was distracted for part of it. About 30 minutes later, his wife told him she was a little upset and bothered that it seemed like he wasn't listening to her. He responded, "You're right. I wasn't listening, and I'm sorry." It's a positive thing that he was happy when his partner started using her voice. It shows he cares about her individuation and not just how he can be served.

Now, if my friend's wife had snapped at him and said, "You idiot, you forgot some towels!" he would have had every right to confront her about the manner in which she was bringing this up. The issue of the towels would still be legitimate, but the way it was brought would be problematic. The same goes for when his wife mentioned being upset about him not listening. Were she to have said, "Hey dumba$$, stop being distracted and listen to me!" he could still acknowledge that she was right about him not listening while also addressing the fact that the way she mentioned it was unacceptable and that she'll need to apologize. Your partner bringing something up poorly does not make their concern illegitimate. With that said, it's vital to address how they brought it up before you discuss their issue. When you don't address your partner's disrespect first, the underlying message you're communicating is that it's okay for them to speak to you poorly.

It's great to have a partner who responds positively to you using your voice. But if they're resistant to the new you, you must ensure they understand this is who you are now and that it will mean taking your wishes and ideas into consideration. It's okay if the two of you ultimately decide not to go with your idea. What's not okay is for your partner to be constantly unwilling to even hear or consider your ideas.

You can think of this in terms of brainstorming sessions. If Julie and Jimmy brainstorm together, sometimes they'll go with Julie's idea and sometimes Jimmy's. With every brainstorming session, Julie and Jimmy both put their ideas onto the table, and they're both willing to use whichever idea is most effective, fun, practical, or satisfies whatever the end goal is. Neither Julie nor Jimmy is invested in being seen as the one who always has the best idea. That's not important to them. What's important to them is using whichever idea makes the most sense, whether that's Jimmy's or Julie's.

Likewise, whenever a decision needs to be made in your partnership, a brainstorming session will commence, though you may call it something else. You and your partner will both put your ideas out there before deciding which one makes the most sense. This applies to big decisions like which city to move to and small decisions like which restaurant to eat at tonight. If you genuinely aren't that invested in a particular decision, like where to eat or what movie to watch, it's okay to let your partner choose. But regarding decisions you care about, insist on your perspective being considered. Hopefully, you won't have to insist—hopefully, your partner will value your input. But if you've been in a pattern of keeping your voice silent for a long time, you may need to show them you're serious by insisting they hear you out and discuss your view of the situation.

When using your voice, it's important to maintain an awareness of the psychological child within you. Consider this question:

Who's not using their voice?

You might answer, "Me. I'm not using my voice." That's true in a sense, but it leaves out an important detail. It's the child consciousness within you who hasn't developed her voice. The adult within you has a voice. You know this, intellectually speaking. You know you can go up to anyone and say anything you want. Except, you don't because there's a fearful part of you. That fearful part is the inner child. The inner child is afraid because he was never taught to use his voice. She was never taught that it's okay to have needs and stand up for those needs. Instead, she was shamed. He was squashed, emotionally speaking.

There might be a moment when you're aware of a need, wish, desire, or something else you want to communicate to your partner. Initially, you think, *Yes, I would like them to know this!* Over the next few seconds, minutes, hours, or days, you talk yourself out of saying it to your partner. The inner child has spoken. She has said, *No, I'm too scared to tell them.* Next, you'll have to rationalize your decision not to communicate this need or wish to your partner, so you tell yourself something like, *I'll be a good spouse and keep the peace.* Or *I don't want to burden my partner with this, so I won't mention it.* Or [take a moment to self-reflect and insert a rationalization you've used to prevent yourself from communicating something that was important to you].

You tell yourself you're doing the right thing by not communicating this point of interest when in reality, you're being driven by the inner child. I underwent intensive therapy starting at 25. There was much to address, from PTSD, major depression, and more. One area to be addressed was toxic family dynamics. My therapist recommended a three-month detox from my parents. This meant no interaction with them for three months. He had been recommending this for at least two years, but I put it off. I wasn't prepared to do it until I realized just how much the family dynamics were negatively affecting me. Every time I interacted with them, it turned crazy, and I was left to emotionally spiral, nosedive, and crash.

The time came for me to commence the three-month detox. Because this was a *conscious choice*, part of the plan involved telling them in person. Many people do a pseudo-detoxification from their parents. This usually looks like just not reaching out much or maybe ignoring their calls and messages but without the parents knowing what's happening. This isn't effective because much of the plan is predicated around using your voice to tell them exactly what you're doing and then processing the feelings that arise in you after telling them. To clarify, I mean processing those feelings with your therapist, journal, and personal support system, not with your parents. If they were capable of processing issues with you, you wouldn't have a need for time away. Simply pulling away isn't using your voice. It can be more like hiding out, reinforcing the inner child's old pattern of hiding.

My therapist made it very clear this three-month detox wasn't about revenge on my parents. It wasn't about saying, "You treated me poorly in such and such ways, so now I'm not talking to you for three months. Take that!" No, it wasn't about that at all. It was about, "I need time to sort out my mental health and emotional healing. For me, part of doing that is going to involve spending three months away from having contact with you." They partially understood that I had to do this for my mental health, but I don't think they completely understood. However, whether they understood or not, the dynamic between us went from child-parent to adult-adult after the detox period. If you allow yourself to remain beneath someone's thumb, whether the agreement is conscious (I knowingly let you make all the decisions and treat me any way you want) or unconscious (I'm telling myself it has to be this way for various rationalized reasons), the person or people whose thumb you're under will perceive you as a child. In perceiving you as a child, they'll interact with you accordingly.

For clarification, the purpose of a detox from your parents or caregivers is to experience what it's like without their regular influence in your life. It detaches you from the patterns you've been engulfed in since childhood. Once I experienced what life was like without the interactions I was having with my parents, I knew I would never go back to how things were. Either they would interact with respect and care, or there wouldn't be a relationship. Many parents are genuinely well-intended and wouldn't want to knowingly hurt their child. I count myself lucky that my parents were willing to rethink how they interacted with me. However, if they wouldn't rethink our relationship and continued to treat me poorly, there wouldn't have been much of a relationship aside from birthday and holiday well wishes.

After experiencing what it was like without the dysfunctional interactions, there was no going back for me.

I shared that piece of my life to highlight which internal voice I was using. At our last session before I initiated the detox with my parents, my therapist reminded me, "Don't go in there and talk to them as a child. When you tell them what you're going to do, speak to them as a mutual adult. Don't let the inner child run the show." You might find safety in interacting with your partner or others in your life from the space of the inner child. It's familiar. In my case, the child may have said to my parents, "Is it okay if I take three months away from you?" As an adult, you claim your personal authority while respecting the personal authority of others.

~

This issue of personal authority can get twisted. Many Instagram therapists say, "Claim your authority!" while leaving the key word "personal" out of it. Some people think this means they're now empowered to go around telling others what to do, and it never works. From there, you either become frustrated and get more aggressive, or you become deflated, abandoning your personal authority altogether.

Personal authority means you have authority over one person: you. A twisted attempt at claiming authority sounds like, "You can't talk to me that way anymore. You have to stop." Claiming personal authority sounds like, "I don't like it when you talk to me that way. Please stop." When they speak to you that way again, you might say, "I tried telling you. Since you ignored me, I won't be around for a week." In this example, personal authority respects the other person's right to choose whether they'll continue talking to you that way. If they choose to continue being disrespectful, you assert your personal authority to not be around them. Don't waste time trying to get them to change. Make a request, and if they don't honor the request, assert your personal authority. The goal is to use as little force as needed. If they don't take you seriously, increase the consequence. If they still don't take you seriously, increase the consequence incrementally until you cut them off. There will be a few people you'll have to cut off, but for the most part, you'll be surprised at how many respect your personal authority. If the person will have an open and honest conversation about the issue, wonderful. But remember, as Don Miguel Ruiz says, "If people say one thing but do another, you're lying to yourself if you don't listen to their actions."

Interestingly, a relationship requires both people. If only one person's voice is heard, if only one person is considered, it's not a relationship, as there's no *relating* going on. Remember that relating means a mutual concern and celebration of what matters to each person. If both people aren't celebrating the other and caring about what matters to the other, what exists is at best a functional agreement, not a relationship.

As you develop your voice, remember to speak as the adult, not the inner child. Claim personal authority over yourself, not authority over others. And remember: You, your voice, needs, opinions, and desires are a vital component of your partnership.

Relationship Skill #4
Own Your Therapeutic Insights

Instead of using your therapist as a scapegoat, take ownership of what you know is best for you.

"My therapist said I need to . . ."

Saying such a thing may be keeping you in a childlike role within your relationship.

As a high school track athlete, I tweaked my ankle playing around with the hurdles (I was not a hurdler), and there was a relay meet the next day. It was the type of injury you could push through and still compete with, but there would be a risk of making it worse. I didn't want to risk making it worse, especially since it wasn't an important meet. If it were districts, regionals, or states, I likely would have competed on it. But with the second half of the season approaching, I wanted to be healthy all the way through. Sometimes, letting yourself rest for a few days can be the difference between a nagging long-term issue and a short-term issue.

I talked to my dad about my ankle, and he agreed that it'd be better to rest it and resume training the following week. I showed up to the bus the next morning without my jersey or track spikes. Coach A. asked what was going on, and I explained that I injured my ankle and wouldn't be running at the meet. Coach A. was clearly unhappy. He wanted me to run that day and was debating my stance. Finally, I said, "My dad said he's going to be mad if I run today." The coach shook his head and became quiet. I wasn't lying, as my dad actually did say that.

Looking back on this, I would have called my coach the previous evening to let him know in advance I wouldn't be running. It's not cool to cancel plans last minute when you know the day or night before something could be wrong. In my work with clients today, when a client says, "I have to cancel today. I wasn't feeling well yesterday. I thought I might feel better today, but I don't feel any better," they still get charged for the session. This policy works because I hold myself to the same standard in that if I cancel in under 24 hours, that client gets a discount at the following session, equivalent to the cancellation fee I charge them if they cancel in under 24 hours.

At any rate, I settled whether I'd be running at the relay meet by telling the coach what my dad said. I didn't have the internal substance to own my wish to sit out that day for myself.

To clarify, there's nothing wrong with you and your partner conversing about what you're learning in therapy. If your therapist's name is Sarah, you might say, "Well, Sarah thinks . . ." or "Sarah said . . ." or "Sarah brought to my attention that . . ." This is healthy for casual conversation. But regarding big decisions, don't look to fall back onto an authority figure other than yourself.

If you and your therapist talk about you removing yourself for 20 minutes the next time your partner engages in name-calling, don't say, "My therapist said to remove myself from you when you say that, so I'm going in the other room." This means nothing to your partner. Well, it means *something*, but nothing helpful to the relationship. It will certainly not create respect. When you phrase it that way, your partner probably thinks you're just blindly following your therapist's advice. Are you? Your partner may already experience you as someone who hasn't claimed their personal authority, and this will cement that more strongly. When you say, "My therapist told me to . . ." you make it sound as if it's not a decision you're taking ownership of.

Your therapist was trying to offer you ways of handling toxic and dysfunctional interactions with your partner. If you believe within yourself that your therapist's idea is useful, use your personal authority to adopt it. The next time your partner is disrespectful, say, "I'm going to step away for 20 minutes because I don't like how you're speaking to me. I'm going in the other room. I'll be back after 20 minutes, and we'll try this conversation again but without the name-calling." Now your partner can see you as someone who exerts their personal authority.

Many therapists are hesitant to give advice. They're interested in holding space for you to talk and guiding you through processing your emotions and traumas. The risk with giving advice, as many therapists see it, is that you'll come back and say, "You told me to do such and such and it didn't work. This is your fault." I think advice is an important part of therapy, especially with certain clients. If you were raised in a dysfunctional family where nobody communicated about their feelings, you will need advice on how to do that. If you're not familiar with dream interpretation, you will need advice in terms of what your dreams are trying to tell you. If you're depressed and have no idea how to cope, you will need advice on how to move toward wellness.

If you're in need of advice in a specific area, but you don't think the advice your therapist offers is relevant, it's time to claim your personal authority and find a different therapist. You can simply say, "Thank you for working with me, but today will be my last appointment." If they ask you why and you don't want to say why, you can respond, "I don't want to go into much detail about that." Also, there's nothing wrong with saying, "The work we're doing isn't resonating with me anymore, but I'm appreciative of the time we've worked together." Between sharing why you're ending the therapeutic relationship and not sharing that information, either way is okay. It's your choice. While there will usually be elements of friendship in therapy, your therapist is firstly a resource who you pay to make use of, not a friend. Even if your therapist cares deeply for you, it would be a disservice to you if they allowed themselves to cross over into friendship instead of maintaining their role as a resource for you. As a resource, they can remain objective and see clearly (although not all therapists see clearly, as some get caught up in their own projections). As a friend, biases inevitably come into play. Positive biases usually feel good to the ego but don't always serve the best interest of your deepest self.

The key is that when you find a therapist you click with (or clergy, friend, mentor, coach, etc.), make conscious acknowledgments with yourself about trying out their advice. You can say to yourself, "I understand that advice can work for some people but not other people. I'm taking responsibility for making the decision to implement the advice I was offered. I've considered the advice and I've decided, under my own power, it's worth trying."

Don't put yourself in the position of being viewed as a blind follower. Think of yourself as a resourceful person who went out and found someone who may have solutions to your problems. Solutions will be offered and utilized only because you went out and found this person for help and because you've decided their potential solutions resonate with you and are worth trying.

53

Relationship Skill #5
The Four Steps of Making Up

Instead of acting like nothing happened, strengthen your relationship by making up.

When you've done something wrong, do you know how to make up?

There are two general types of wrongdoing. The first is overt wrongdoing. This involves something you did. For example, purposely insulting your partner about a known sensitive area is an overt act of wrongdoing, as is breaking a known agreement between the two of you. The second type of wrongdoing involves a lack of action. This could look like not giving your partner any attention. You didn't do anything bad, right? You're not a bad person for not giving your partner attention, but it still hurts them and the overall health of the relationship. Another example would be being mostly passive in your relationship. You're not doing anything wrong per se, but your lack of engagement in the relationship harms it.

Regardless of the type of wrongdoing, making up will look similar. Making up involves four steps:

1. Acknowledgment

2. Admission of Wrongdoing

3. Apology

4. Closing the Gap

Acknowledgment

Simply, acknowledgment is stating what you did. Using the examples in the previous paragraph, it would sound like, "I made a comment about an area that I knew would bother you," or "I haven't given you much attention for the last two weeks."

There's nothing fancy about this step. You don't have to have any special skills other than identifying the hurtful action or lack of action and putting it into a clear and simple statement.

Admission of Wrongdoing

This step is also simple but not always easy. Admission sounds like, "It was wrong of me to do that," or "I was wrong for doing that." Many people have difficulty using the words "I" and "wrong" in the same sentence, but it's necessary to effectively make up.

So far, you've acknowledged what you did and admitted it was wrong to do it.

Apology

An apology has two parts. First, a statement of regret, and second, saying the word sorry.

To state your regret, you can say, "I state my regret." False. Do not say, "I state my regret." That was taken from an episode of *The Office* where Dwight Schrute was ordered to formally apologize to his coworkers.

Let your partner know you regret what you did or didn't do. I've heard people say, "I'm sorry, but I would do it again." So, what you're saying is that you're not sorry. You're saying the word sorry, but you're not actually sorry for what happened. You wish the person wasn't hurt by it, but you saw it as a necessary act. To be sorry, there must be a sense of regret. A statement of regret sounds like, "I regret saying that" or "I regret that I haven't been doing that."

Next, the s-word. If you say, "I apologize," hopefully, you just lightly bumped into someone at the grocery store or something else inconsequential. Saying "I apologize" is a social norm, but it only applies to basically harmless deeds in social settings. Showing up three minutes late to a work meeting would be another example of when "I apologize" is appropriate. If you show up 20 minutes late and you're the primary presenter, "I apologize" won't cut it. If you carelessly bump into someone's leg at the store with your cart, causing them to buckle down from the pain, "I apologize" isn't commensurate with the mistake. Saying "I apologize" is a way of maintaining social grace in minor situations.

Many people are deeply affected when the s-word comes out of their mouth. It's like their mouth is on fire when they say it, so they must lessen the pain of the word. Saying "I apologize" is one way of doing that. Another way is saying, "I'm sorry you feel that way." This is not making up with someone, it's an avoidance of personal responsibility for your hurtful act or lack of action. The point is not to be sorry for how your partner feels but to be sorry for what you did or didn't do.

To use an extreme example, imagine a formerly physically abusive man who wants to turn his life around. His 26-year-old daughter says, "Dad, I'm still feeling hurt from the times I saw you punch mom and push her down." In response, he says, "I'm sorry you feel that way." The only appropriate response from the father is a version of, "I did that, I was wrong, I regret my actions, and I'm sorry. I'm so sorry. I know me doing that impacted you deeply." Now *that's* taking personal responsibility. With personal responsibility, you're sorry for the action or lack of action you took. You can feel sad that the other person is hurt by it, and that's important too. You can say, "I feel sad that you're hurt by what I did, and I'm sorry for doing it. I know it was wrong."

Be careful being too hard on people making a genuine effort. If someone says they're sorry for what they did or they regret having done what they did, that's a decent apology. I don't think that type of apology is going to have the same restorative impact as the steps outlined here. However, if your father, who never shared an emotion in his entire life, says something like that, it's truly a good effort given his capabilities. With that said, I don't believe "I'm sorry you feel that way" is ever an honest attempt to apologize. It's more like saying, "I'm never going say what I did was wrong, but if you feel bad about it, I'll sprinkle a few drops of pity your way so you'll drop the subject already."

To get nuanced on this subject, if your partner shares about a difficult time they're going through at work and it's not related to you, you can say, "I'm sorry you're so stressed out about this. I don't want you to feel that way. But I understand why you do. It sounds like a hard situation." The word "sorry" is primarily related to ownership of wrongdoing, but occasionally, like in this example, it can be used to express sadness over seeing a loved one in pain. However, it's clearer to say, "I feel sad you're so stressed about this." But if you're the one who inflicted the pain through wrongdoing, a useful rule of thumb is to not tell them you're sorry for the way they feel. Rather, word it in a way that takes ownership of what you did, i.e., what I did was wrong, and I'm sorry for doing it.

Closing the Gap

Consider the phrase "making up." In football, if a wide receiver is running down the field with the ball and a defender is five yards behind him, the defender must *make up* the five-yard gap to reach his goal of tackling the ball runner. As another example, if your goal is to do 1,200 pushups in a month, you might do 40 per day. If you skip a day, you'll have to *make up* for the pushups that weren't done that day, or you won't reach the goal of 1,200. In both cases, a gap needs to be filled.

In some relational situations, the gap can be made up through acknowledgment, admission of wrongdoing, and apology. If you use a nasty tone of voice at your partner, the A-triplets might be enough. To use the example from earlier, if you purposely make cruel comments to your partner about an area of their being that's very sensitive and challenging for them, the three A's might not be enough to close the gap. To be clear, they need you to acknowledge what you did, admit it was wrong, and apologize. From there, if this was a major hurt, more will be needed. A gap in the relationship was caused, and something must make up for it.

It used to be common for stores to have "You Break It, You Buy It" signs. If you're looking at a vase and you drop it, that vase is gone. The store owner had purchased the vase using money, and now that money won't be recouped. There's now a financial gap in the books. The gap can be made up by you paying for the broken vase.

As an example of closing the gap, you might say, "I'm still so sorry for what I said. We usually take turns grocery shopping each week, and I know you don't like to do it. For the next six weeks, I'll do it every week." Be sure your "make up" activity is commensurate with what happened.

Don't use things that would typically be a healthy part of a relationship in the first place. Don't use sex or buying flowers as a makeup activity. Doing so comes with a sense of only doing it because you're in the hole with your partner right now. And that IS why you're doing it. Your partner likely wishes you would be more sexually interested as a normal part of the relationship or buy them flowers regularly. In closing the gap, avoid areas that would be part of a healthy relationship in the first place, as you'll only be highlighting the fact that they're not a normal part of the relationship. This will prevent a conversation that sounds like, "You only buy me flowers after you've done something hurtful."

When it comes to something like grocery shopping, it's understood that it's not a well-liked activity (that doesn't apply across the board). As such, it carries more weight in closing the gap after wrongdoing. Don't turn yourself into a permanent indentured servant to your partner, but it is okay to temporarily put in some sweat equity after a particularly hurtful interaction.

In *Modern Family*, there's an episode where Claire calls Gloria a gold digger. Claire wants to make up for her mean comment, and Gloria suggests she jump in the pool with her clothes on. Claire does it and Gloria finally accepts her apology. This isn't to suggest you go jump into a pool, off a roof, or lie down on an anthill full of fire ants. The point is that Claire's words alone weren't enough to bring her and Gloria back into a positive connection. An action was required to close the gap caused by Claire's words. Especially regarding major hurts or repeat hurts that are similar, be willing to put in some sweat equity beyond only your words to show your partner you want to close the gap you created.

What if your partner takes advantage of your attempts to close the gap? If they're genuinely interested in a good relationship, they won't be interested in taking advantage, as it will harm the relationship further. A willingness and desire to forgive from their end is part of the equation, too. For example, if you do the grocery shopping for the next six weeks and your partner isn't yet in a good space, you can try doing more. But if 12 weeks have gone by and they're no closer to being in a good space with you although you are sorry, have expressed that sorrow, and you've tried to close the gap, maybe A) the attempt to close the gap isn't commensurate with the harm inflicted (in which case you'll have to reevaluate this area), or B) the experience has brought up other issues for your partner. It may remind them of something from childhood, such as a trauma or emotional wound. In such cases, your partner will need to address this through their own healing work. You can say, "I'm still as sorry as I was, I truly regret what I said, I feel so upset that I said what I did, I've tried to show you my sorrow by putting in sweat equity, but I can't make my apology any stronger than I have."

In some instances, hurt happens in relationships that can't be repaired. For example, say your partner was burned on the entire left side of their face as a child. Kids made fun of them at school. Everywhere your partner goes, people stare. Anyone they meet can hardly look your partner in the eyes because they're distracted by the burn. Then, in a moment of anger, you say things about your partner's burned face that put you in the same category as the kids who made fun and all the people who have treated your partner like a lesser human because of how

60

they look. Such a thing has the potential to permanently rupture the relationship. Maybe they could forgive but never trust again. Maybe they can only forgive from a distance but not when in close proximity. Regarding your partnership, it's important to hold it in a place of honor, never taking it for granted because even the most forgiving person in the world still has limits. Be cautious not to put your partner in a place of having to test the limits of their ability to forgive.

Relationship Skill #6
Forgiveness Has Limits

Instead of taking your partner for granted, make it easier for them to forgive and reconnect.

A colleague who runs workshops for people raised in dysfunctional families often says, "I believe in forgiveness, always. But sometimes you can only forgive from 300 miles away." Some relationships become so dysfunctional and painful that you can't be around one another without triggering fear, pain, anxiety, frustration, and anger.

If you were sexually abused by a caregiver, you may have found it in your heart to forgive them, but this doesn't mean you have to want to spend time with them. On the other end of the forgiveness spectrum, if a caregiver raised their voice at you occasionally, you may not have liked it, but you can forgive it and still form an adult relationship with them.

You will need to forgive your partner often, but there are different levels of forgiveness. It's human nature to make a rude comment or use an unfriendly tone from time to time. If your partner is willing to promptly acknowledge when this has happened and apologize, I suspect you'd have a high willingness to forgive and get back into a state of positive connection. But with something like your partner having had an affair, it's not a matter of whether you'll forgive them. For your own good, you need to forgive. The real question is whether you're able and willing to get back into a positive connection with your partner.

With the affair example, maybe your partner decides they're willing to go to therapy and other recovery groups. They make an effort to alter your relationship for the better. In this case, you might be willing to get back into connection with them in addition to forgiving them. Alternatively, you might decide that while you understand they're just a fragile human like you and everybody else, you aren't willing to get back into a state of connection after the affair, though they're willing to work on themselves. Or you might wish you could get back into a state of connection with your partner, and you might try and try, but your body and emotions say no. A client comes to mind who wanted to get back into a state of connection with her partner but couldn't make it happen. This client described that her partner broke promises and hadn't communicated about issues in the relationship, instead opting to withdraw. These issues took place multiple times over a couple of years. This client said she had made an effort to communicate and had brought up the agreements that had been broken, but her husband was unresponsive to her rectification attempts. "I always thought I could keep it up for years," she described. "I thought I could just continue sitting down and talking over and over for an indefinite period of time until he started communicating and keeping our agreements. But at some point along the way, my heart began saying *no*." She described that her inner critic was telling her she was supposed to work it out with her spouse, but deep down she knew she had made every effort possible and that her heart was no longer in it. She wished she still wanted to work on the relationship, but after everything that had happened over a long period, her deeper self said no. She kept it up a while longer, even after her body began saying no. As a result of fighting against her own body, she became sick from the stress of continually trying to work it out. Her emotional brakes were on, but she kept pressing the gas pedal. She said, "There was a point when I could admit I didn't want to do it anymore, but I was still trying to force myself into wanting to do it. Because of this, I was constantly in a state of internal tension." Stress that lasts a few days or weeks is manageable. Constant stress over several months or more can lead to health issues.

The Difference Between Forgiveness and a State of Connection
The distinction between forgiveness and entering back into a state of connection was mentioned in the previous section. Let's look more deeply at the difference between forgiveness and a state of connection.

Forgiveness is when you say: I choose to look at the person who committed the hurtful act as a hurting, confused human be-cause I know when I do something hurtful, it's because I'm a hurting, confused human, too. I understand that when some-one does something hurtful, even if there was an intentional component to it, they don't fully understand what they're do-ing. If they did, there would only be love. None of us fully un-derstand what we're doing. If we did, there would only be love in the world.

Entering back into a state of connection looks like: I will open my heart to this person once again.

Some clients describe their spouse or ex-partner as a monster. "He's an evil monster," is what they'll say. People say this when they think they're only allowed to be upset or angry at someone if they can prove the person is evil. Such people must concoct a story that the other person knows exactly what they're doing. While that could be true to an extent, the logic of it falls apart every single time.

Usually, people don't understand their toxic behavior. They're not purposely singling you out. If you must see them as evil to validate your feelings, then you'll tell yourself they're doing it on purpose. You're allowed to feel how you feel about a person, even if they're a confused, hurting person like the rest of us.

In other cases, some people are purposefully manipulative. However, this only goes so far. You might have a parent who purposely manipulated everyone in the family against one another. Maybe your spouse is abusing you and purposely manipulating you into believing it's your fault that they punched you. In these cases, it's easy to call the person an evil monster. Afterall, they're doing it on purpose. They still don't completely know what they're doing.

Even if they're purposely manipulating you, they don't know what they're doing. You can't hurt someone else without first hurting yourself. They think they're oppressing you while making themselves happy. For every external way they oppress you, they're psychologically oppressing themselves in an equal manner. You have become the object of their projection. Because they can't control themselves emotionally, they're trying to control and suppress an external person. Their emotions are so painful that they project them outward because they can't feel them without crumbling. So, yes, this person is purposely controlling. However, do they understand what they're doing? The answer is a resounding no. If they understood, they'd let themselves fall into the abyss of pain and darkness that is their interior life. Experiencing their own dark misery is the only way such a person will change. Until they experience it, they'll continue to project their pain onto an external person. They know they're trying to control you, but they don't know why they're doing it. They might have intellectual, surface-level reasons and rationalizations as to why, but they don't understand the deepest driving factors. They're out of touch with their deepest self, and that leads to an attempt to control their experience of life by controlling other people, which never works.

With this subject, there's always the issue of "So you're saying I should stay with my partner who physically abuses me?" Not even close. Seek the support you need and leave immediately. Get the hell out of there. What I am saying is that even in extreme cases, people aren't evil monsters, they're confused, hurting human beings.

This is hard for people because when they hear the words "confused and hurting human beings" their empathy is triggered. "I'm an empath," they say, "and if I see them as confused and hurting, I can't abandon them." That's not what an empath is. An empath is someone with sensitive perceptions about others. Being an empath does not involve letting others cross your boundaries. A codependent person needs to be needed. Codependent people let their boundaries get tromped. They believe they're obligated to help and support anyone in pain, regardless of whether that person treats them with respect. A well-developed empath knows better than anyone that you can't make people change and that continually supporting someone who is abusive isn't support at all, it's enabling. A codependent person thinks they have to stay in the face of abuse and endless pain. A developed empath has a heart of wisdom that guides them to use their gift with people open to it as a gift, not as a necessary task under the threat of hostility if you stop giving. Be cautious not to confuse codependent behaviors with being an empath.

Someone can be a confused, hurting human *and* you can choose not to enter back into connection with that person. When people think they're only allowed to not enter back into connection if a person is an evil monster, they get stuck. "He punched me in the face, but look, now I see a glimpse of his humanity." When they see the humanity of their abuser, they can no longer see him as a monster. Then they get hit again several weeks later, but something once again brings out their humanity. Seeing someone's humanity is not cause to stay. Often, glimpsing their humanity causes your heart to open back up to the person. But in cases of abuse or issues that persist beyond your ability to handle the stress of, you can both acknowledge their humanity and step away. It doesn't have to be one or the other. Seeing them as an evil monster is not a prerequisite to stepping away.

Being in a state of connection means you're choosing to open yourself up to being influenced and impacted by the other person. If you open yourself to someone who communicates with you, expresses appreciation, and embraces you, you'll be affected by that because you opened your heart. If your heart isn't open, even if they do all of those uplifting things, it won't impact you. Do you find you have trouble being affected by the kindness of your partner? If so, you'll need to explore why your heart is closed off. Is it because of an unresolved relationship issue, or is it because of old traumas and emotional wounds you haven't addressed? If it's the latter, any possibility of emotional intimacy will scare or trigger you. *Hauntings* by James Hollis is a great book for gaining clarity on whether your past is affecting your present relationship. If you ask me, it's an awful book title. But the content will be eye-opening.

If you open your heart back up to someone who can't or won't keep agreements that were made (or at least come to you and discuss that they won't be upholding the agreement and then work with you to find another mutually agreeable path forward), you're going to be impacted by that in some way. The way you're affected might be different after the tenth time than after the first or second. There's usually a willingness to open back up to a person after a few missteps. However, when patterns continue over long periods, something deep within you might simply say no. From there, no matter how hard you try, maybe you can't force your heart back open without doing emotional violence to yourself.

Regarding forgiveness, ask yourself, "Do I see this person as a confused, hurting human being?" If you don't, then you might be validating your feelings by telling yourself they're a monster. Your feelings are valid even when dealing with a confused, hurting human. Next, ask yourself, "Am I willing to put myself back into a state of connection with this confused, hurting human being?"

Again, we're all confused, hurting humans. We all must offer one another grace, otherwise, nobody would ever be in relationship at all. However, after you've undergone much thought and reflection as well as professional consulting, you may determine that the best course of action is to forgive a certain confused, hurting human from afar and not enter back into a state of connection with them.

As one last note on this subject, consider the ways your partner has been hurt by you. Consider the ways you've been hurt by your partner. Assuming irreparable acts haven't been committed, reflect on how amazing, how wonderful it is that you can open your heart back up to them and they open theirs back up to you. It's truly a beautiful thing to contemplate. Don't take it for granted.

Forgiveness is a necessary part of relationships. Without it, partnerships can't survive. Yet, forgiveness can only go so far and does not equal being in a state of positive connection.

Relationship Skill #7
Keep Your Word

Instead of speaking empty words, follow through.

This is a basic skill that few people live by. If you're into Instagram therapy, the prevailing viewpoint is: I can change my mind whenever I want to. While technically true, it looks only at one side of the coin while ignoring the other.

On one side of the coin, you *are* allowed to change your mind whenever you want to. Truly, you are allowed. So, let's say you've decided you'll no longer be following through on a particular agreement. That's your right, and you can exercise that right at any time. The thing about agreements is that they involve another person. With that in mind, let's look at the other side of the coin.

The human being you made an agreement with has feelings and needs as you have feelings and needs. When you decide not to follow through on what you agreed to, how will the other human feel about it? The answer to that depends on a few factors. Did you discuss it with them, communicating your change of heart? Does this happen with most agreements you make with your partner, or is this a one-time and/or rare occurrence? Regarding agreements pertaining to partnerships, how you feel about it and handle it is only one side of the coin. The other side of the coin is the person you made the agreement with. How will not following through affect your partner and thereby the relationship as a whole, as your partner is part of what forms the relationship?

As a general rule, keeping agreements builds and maintains trust. Trust in a relationship is a lot like any body part. As an example, part of my personal trauma history is that as a teenager, I was grabbed by the throat by the athletic director of my school district. I had no tools to handle trauma, so I kept quiet about it, not telling anybody. From there, I developed vocal cord problems. I didn't appreciate the gift of speaking effortlessly until I had vocal cord problems. Similarly, you might not recognize or appreciate the trust within a partnership until it's damaged or gone.

There are cases where keeping your word could have a negative impact on you and your partner. If you're the one who's consistently showing up, following through, and keeping your word while your partner can't or won't keep a single agreement or care about what your wishes are, you continuing to do the work of showing up and keeping your word is likely leaving the realm of support and entering the realm of enabling. In these cases, it's not recommended that you quit showing up. Instead, let them know where you stand. Tell them you will not be doing certain things anymore until they begin to show up in the relationship, too. Doing this will either have the effect of them realizing how much they value you and the relationship, or it will show how much they value their current ways of being, thus not eliciting any change. If they don't change, don't take it personally. Them not changing isn't a reflection of how valuable you are. It reflects how much trauma and pain they're experiencing internally, requiring their defense mechanisms to remain active at any cost. The keyword here is *any* cost. People sometimes like to hope, think, and wish that their marriage, relationship, or children they have together would be valuable enough to motivate a stuck partner into changing. Regarding trauma and the resulting defense mechanisms that inhibit the ability to show up in a relationship, it may have been so painful, emotionally and psychologically speaking, that no external motivator will inspire change.

Write It Down

When you make an agreement or give your word, don't assume you'll remember. Write it down in a planner. Purchase a physical planner specifically for this purpose. "I'll just set a reminder on my phone." You can, but it probably won't work. Phones and other screen devices have so much happening at once, like social media, email, text, and app notifications, that the reminder you set on your phone will more than likely blend in with the rest of the notifications. It'll pop up, you'll swipe it away, and then you'll find yourself saying, "I set the reminder on my phone, and it went off, but then I forgot." This is your relationship, and you have a 50% role in contributing to its quality and health, so why not value it enough to distinguish it from the rest of the daily noise on your phone?

Trust isn't automatic in relationships. It's built. Many people are highly offended if someone doesn't trust them. This is more about their own self-image than it is about the relationship. They want to view themselves as trustworthy, and they'll argue, yell, and defend when their partner is having trouble trusting them.

The reason this issue arises at all is that, as a society, we somehow came to believe that trust comes automatically. If, as a society, we could shift to a belief that trust is built and not automatically present, there would be far fewer issues and hurt egos around trust.

Several years ago, I made plans with a new friend, and it was the first time he and I were getting together. On the day of the plans, he sent a text saying, "Still good for today?" I jokingly responded, "No, I decided to cancel without telling you." He told me he laughed when he saw that message. It was the first and last time he sent a text to confirm getting together. The question here is why did he text me in the first place? He didn't know if I could be trusted to follow through on what I said I would do. Trust doesn't come automatically. It's built and earned.

Being a generally good and nice person doesn't earn trust. Neither does the length of time you know somebody. Trust is built based on specific actions that demonstrate you can be relied upon. In relationships, it's a gift to know someone's word is their bond, while it's an immense burden to constantly question whether someone will keep their word. We become defensive around trust issues because we can't think of ourselves as anything other than trustworthy. The problem with this stance is that issues of greater or lesser degree inevitably arise in relationships. If you and your partner have an agreement of no name-calling in your relationship, trust was broken whether one of you calls the other a jerk or whether one of you pinpoints a specific, self-conscious area within the other and exploits it (remember the example of the face burn from earlier). The difference is that trust can potentially be rebuilt quickly and with minimal effort in the first case ("I'm sorry, that was wrong of me to say that and to break our agreement") but will be much more difficult in the second case. Both cases were examples of a lack of trustworthiness, but the degree of trust broken will largely determine how quickly it can be rebuilt, if at all.

If you view yourself as trustworthy, that's great. Maybe. The reason it's a maybe is that if you *need* to view yourself as trustworthy, it makes you less likely to acknowledge and rebuild trust when you inevitably make a mistake. You'll probably feel ashamed and want to avoid the issue. Most people who commit hurtful acts would consider themselves good people. Don't give so much importance to a self-identity of being a good or trustworthy person. People don't care what your self-identity is, they care if you show up and follow through. Don't think, "I'm trustworthy," instead, take actions that build trust. Don't think, "I'm a good person," instead, take actions that are good for others and yourself.

Someone might say, "Self-identity matters because it gives you a sense of who you are." Okay, that's fair. Consider this as a compromise between the extremes of throwing self-identity out the window and grasping it so tightly it cuts your hand: Hold onto your self-identity loosely. You like to view yourself as a trustworthy person. Who wouldn't? But are you holding onto that as part of who you are so tightly that you can't acknowledge when you've committed a hurtful action and broken your partner's trust? If you can't discuss your partner having difficulty trusting you without defending yourself like your life depends on it, chances are you're holding onto the identity of being a trustworthy person too tightly. Loosen the grip.

My partner and I were once sitting on the couch having a disagreement. My leg was resting on a footstool, and during the disagreement, I became frustrated and shoved the footstool with my foot. It was a small and light footstool, weighing 2-3 pounds. It slid a foot or two across the carpet. From my perspective, it was a light, minor shove, using about 10% of the force my leg could produce. However, it upset my partner to see me shove the footstool out of frustration with my foot. That night, she said, "I don't feel safe around you, so I'm sleeping in the other room."

I could have responded, "Are you kidding? I shoved it with like 10% of my power. It was barely anything. It's just a dinky, light footstool. A fly landing on it could knock it over. Now you think I'm a danger to you? You think I'm not safe? I can't believe you think I'd hurt you somehow. You must be crazy to even think that. Do you even know me at all? How could you think that about me?" That's how I could have responded.

I responded by saying, "I understand. I want you to do what you need to do to take care of yourself." I was happy she was using her voice and taking care of herself. The next day, we talked through the issue. If I had responded defensively, her trust in me would have plummeted.

Regarding trust, remember that you're allowed to change your mind about anything. With that in mind, being allowed doesn't mean it won't impact the person on the other side of the agreement. Therefore, make agreements carefully and after much thought, as breaking them can quickly shatter trust.

~

When an agreement must be broken, go to the person you made it with and discuss the topic. Avoid enacting your change of mind before discussing it with your partner. Acting on your change of mind before letting your partner know will likely be viewed as a betrayal. If you discuss it with them first, they may still be hurt, but it won't be viewed as a total betrayal. Talking to them first will save you the repair work of a betrayal.

Being up front and honest about going back on your word grants them the ability to respond how they see fit. If you don't let them know you're going back on your word and they think you will still follow through on the agreement, they'll likely feel angry and frustrated that you didn't inform them. They were relating to you as if the agreement was still on. Now the specific date has come, or some time has passed, and they realize you don't intend to follow through. Give your partner the gift of autonomy—they have a right to respond to your change of mind how they wish in the same way you have the right to change your mind. Don't keep it from them. Would you rather deal with honest challenges in a truthful relationship, or keep things from one another as long as possible, then deal with them when the bubble inevitably pops?

As an example, you and your partner discuss getting a new car. You have different tastes but agree that a Ford SUV will meet your style, functionality, and price needs. Then, one day you're out and come across a nice Subaru. The opportunity won't last, so you jump on it. While you may personally think it's a better car for the same price as the Ford, when you open the garage to show your partner, all they'll see is a big, shiny betrayal with all-wheel drive.

If it's not worth sticking to your agreement, what was the point of the time and energy put into researching and discussing vehicles together? What was the point of the long conversations? Your partner might even like the Subaru more than the Ford, but do you know what they won't like? That they couldn't be secure in your word.

Assuming the vehicle has a return policy, a simple attempt at contacting your partner with a couple of phone calls and a text could make all the difference. You can say, "I tried calling and texting, but you weren't available. I went ahead and bought it, knowing it has a 7-day return policy. So, if you don't like it, we'll return it." The attempts at contacting your partner and your willingness to return it will shift the dynamic from betrayal (i.e., we made an agreement that was blatantly broken) to surprise or irritation (i.e., I'm a little pissed off, but we'll sort this out).

~

When it comes to keeping your word, there are levels of degree. If you told your partner you'd be ready at 11:00 am but weren't ready until 11:10, you didn't keep your word. If this happens once every few months, it will likely not be a major issue. In such cases, your partner may accept this flaw in you. It's part of how you behave; they accept that and won't ask you to change. If it happens multiple times per week, now you're asking more of your partner. Essentially, you're asking them to look beyond you breaking your own word multiple times a week. This can create a real chip in the trust between you. In such cases, I'm not surprised when I see a partner accept this for a few months or even years, but eventually, they become frustrated and upset about it. Small issues like this can be repaired fairly easily by simply being ready when you said you'd be ready.

What about larger issues? Sometimes, broken agreements are so life-altering that repair isn't possible. For example, say you and your partner agree you want kids. Once you're married, one partner decides they no longer want kids. But the other one has always wanted children. If they knew their partner wouldn't want kids, they never would have married them. This is a big, life-altering change of mind. Not only for the one changing their mind, but also for their partner who still wants kids.

Another example could be you and your partner both wanting to move. You agree to an area you both like before you get married, then, once you're married, one of you no longer wants to move. Moving is still important to the other partner, and they don't want to settle where the two of you live. The one who still wants to move would never have entered into the marriage if they knew the other would no longer be willing to move. The examples of wanting kids or moving someplace new are life-altering matters, whereas running a few minutes late can be irritating, sometimes very irritating, but it's likely not life-altering.

In life-altering cases, the respectable thing would be for the person who is no longer following up on their agreement to give an out to the other partner. To go into a marriage or domestic partnership having both agreed to have kids and then the partner who changes their mind expecting the other partner to live with it is a mighty steep expectation. It's an unreasonable expectation to ask someone who has always wanted kids to simply be okay with not pursuing that, especially if having kids was mutually agreed upon before the marriage. The same applies to moving. If you both agreed to move before the marriage or domestic partnership took place and someone changed their mind, it's a lot to expect the one who still wants to move to suck it up and be okay with not moving. In these cases, offering an out is the only way to potentially save the relationship.

You can say, "I know we agreed to have kids. Now, I've changed my mind and will not be upholding my side of the agreement.

It's unfair of me to expect you to be okay with that. Since this is such a life-altering change of mind, I completely understand if you want to leave this relationship so you can pursue having children." Even if they decide to leave, they'll respect you for this. It's better for them to leave on a note of mutual respect than to stay and have lost all respect for you because of what you're asking of them. By not pressuring them to "just live with it" no matter how much they don't like it, you won't be viewed as their adversary. They'll be able to look at the situation objectively without seeing you as an enemy to be overcome. There's a big difference between having to *fight* for what they want (fighting against someone who's expecting them to be okay with it) and *simply deciding* (looking at the situation and choosing between two options). Acting as if your change of mind is no big deal or avoiding discussing the matter in hopes it'll go away are not viable solutions, relationally speaking. You might temporarily have a sense of being off the hook, but if your partner is unhappy, it will eventually affect the relationship in ways far worse than respectfully giving them an out ever could. Giving them an out shows you value the agreement and respect them. Expecting them to just go along with your change of mind shows that the agreement didn't mean anything to you and therefore you don't value your partner or your word. Again, this brings us back to whether you'd rather face difficulties openly, honestly, and up front in your partnership or let the bubble expand until it pops. When changing your mind about having kids, giving your partner an out puts the impetus on them. If they stay, it will have been their choice. If you refuse to discuss the issue or honor your partner's autonomy, things might seem okay for a while. But the bubble is growing, and when it pops down the road, there might be so much resentment splattered all over the house that you can't easily clean it up. Now you're in for a complete remodel, costing you tremendous energy and money. Respecting your partner's right to choose up front how they want to respond to your changes of mind can prevent the need for a complete remodel.

Here, I'd like to take a moment to address a common response to this issue of giving your partner an out. A frequent reaction to this concept from people who abide by the Christian faith tradition is, "I'm not going to give my partner permission to leave the relationship even if I break my word in life-altering ways because we made a vow to one another." This is a fair point. Most vows are "for better or for worse," and a spouse breaking their word in a major area would be one of the "for worse" moments. Let's add another element to this line of thinking. Adultery, substance addiction, and abuse are often the only causes for marital separation in this tradition. A vow is a vow, period, and unless one of the aforementioned occurs, there are no grounds for separation. However, many who believe a vow is a vow, period, also believe: "Simply let your yes be yes, and your no, no. Anything more comes from the evil one." Based on this teaching, if two partners make an agreement and one doesn't follow through with the agreement, the one who didn't follow through would do well to engage in honest self-examination, acknowledge their wrongdoing, and seek to repair and make it right as soon as possible. At the same time, many also believe in grace, forgiveness, mercy, and love. The point here is to not take advantage of, or for granted, that your partner made a vow. Let yes or no from your mouth be as important as the wedding vows. Don't take advantage of the fact that, as a person who believes in these principles, your partner must practice grace, mercy, forgiveness, and love, because they can offer you all four of those and still not trust you. As an adult, your role is to take responsibility for being trustworthy. Don't demand your partner keep their vow while they can't rely on a simple yes or no from you. Don't assume your partner will continue to trust you no matter how many times or to what degree you don't keep your word.

When trust is broken, the person whose trust was broken now has to decide: Do I remain in a positive connection, or has the relationship been severed beyond repair? This is something essential to consider with decisions that involve your partner. For some decisions, it's not worth the trust that will be broken. With the car example, on the one hand, getting a nice deal on a car isn't worth the repair work that'll be required of you after the fact if there's no return policy. On the other hand, if there's a return policy available, the issue will still require some repair work, but ultimately it can be reversed if your partner is awfully unhappy with it. As a final example, you might be miserable at your job, but it pays good money, so your partner isn't on board with you starting your own business. Yet, you're miserable day in and day out, and that's no way to live. You might say, "I know you're not on board, I know you're going to be upset, but I'm transitioning out of my job. I don't want to make you unhappy, but this job is eating away at my soul every single day, so I have to do something. I love you, but I can't do this job anymore." There's going to be repair work involved, but it will be worth it because of the immense misery you experience with your job.

As you can see, keeping your agreements—and changing them only after considerable personal reflection and discussion with your partner—can play an enormous role in keeping your relationship stable, positive, and filled with trust.

Relationship Skill #8
Listen to Understand,
Not Just to Respond

Instead of thinking about what you want to say next, listen deeply.

Do you listen just to respond, or do you listen to <u>hear</u>? Interestingly, if you focus less on your response and more on what your partner is saying, your responses will be more on point.

There are three levels of listening. The first is hearing only fragments of what the other person is saying. The second is audibly hearing all the words being spoken by the other person. The third level is truly hearing what the person is saying.

With the first level, you might catch a word here or a word there. If you realize you caught only the tail end of something important, you might have to say, "Wait, what did you say?" Or you might not even acknowledge what the person said. A conversation might look like:

Them: "I was thinking we could look at hiking spots within an hour of here and try one out tomorrow or next weekend. I think it'd be a lot of fun."

You: "Uh huh. Want to watch this movie I found on Netflix?"

Your partner will likely be upset because your response indicates not having heard (or cared about) what they just said.

On the second level, you hear the words. Since you understand English, you can rationally piece together what the words mean. You may not have a sense of connecting with what was said, but you comprehend the sentence.

Them: "I was thinking we could look at hiking spots within an hour of here and try one out tomorrow or next weekend. I think it'd be a lot of fun."

You: "Oh yeah, okay. Let me get the laptop and start looking up some places."

Here, your partner will sense you have heard what they said. They'll be happy their idea is being acknowledged and acted upon.

On the third level, you hear the words and the meaning behind the words. You experience an internal connection with what was said.

Them: "I was thinking we could look at hiking spots within an hour of here and try one out tomorrow or next weekend. I think it'd be a lot of fun."

You: "Sounds like you want to unplug and have fun. Has something stressful been happening, or are you just in a fun mood?"

Wow. Your partner's eyes might light up when they realize how deeply you've heard them. They might share a little bit about what's going on.

Them: "This has been such a rough week at work. I just want to get out in the woods and walk."

You: "I'd love to get out and walk with you. You can tell me about the stress on the ride there." If you really want to show your desire to walk with them, you can give them a hug here. If you're in a playful mood, slip in a one or two-handed booty squeeze after the hug.

Or they might say: "I just really want to get outside in nature. I love being out in nature."

You: "I'd love to do that with you. Let's look up places. I'm excited!" Since this is more playful energy than the energy of your partner being stressed, fake going in for the hug and go right for the two-handed booty squeeze.

Note that your initial response didn't assume to know why they wanted to go hiking. Instead, you inquired about why. This shows interest in them as a person. Inquiring shows interest, whereas jumping to conclusions or assuming you know why your partner wants to go hiking can seem disconnected.

~

Make no mistake: Listening well requires energy. A client has a friend who calls her regularly. The friend asks how she's doing, and they talk about that for a few minutes, usually less than 10. From there, the friend begins talking about her life, and that takes up the next hour. This pattern of my client talking about herself for a few minutes, followed by her friend talking about her life for an hour is consistent. My client says she finds it draining. Have you ever been drained or fatigued after listening to someone talk for a long time? Have you ever had someone in your life who, when they call, you get a sinking feeling in your stomach? *Oh no, that's Judy. This will be a long phone call. I don't have the energy for it.* You might then feel guilty for not wanting to take the phone call.

There are reasons it's draining to listen to someone talk and talk. For one thing, you're making an effort to focus on them and not on anything else. You're not scrolling on your phone and you're keeping your attention on that person and their words. With each word, your brain takes it in and processes the meaning of it. If you're actively attempting to have empathy, you're also doing the emotional work of trying to understand where they're coming from, not becoming attached to your judgments about what they're saying. (We all have judgments. The key is recognizing them without becoming attached to them. Hold your judgments loosely, as becoming attached to them blocks connection.) From an observer's perspective, listening might look like just sitting there quietly, but it takes work, and that's why it's so draining when a conversation is one-sided.

Listening can be draining for two reasons. The first reason is about protecting yourself. If you've been listening attentively for several minutes straight, especially if the talker has no intention of sorting their issue out or looking for solutions, your listening energy is probably close to empty. If this is your partner, you can say, "I'm all listened out. I don't have the energy to hear more." If it's a friend or acquaintance you're not ready to be honest with, you can say, "I have some things I've got to take care of, so got to get going. Bye." However, I recommend having a direct conversation on listening energy with your partner. This is the person you've chosen to share your life with—best to address issues rather than let them stew. It's worth being transparent and sorting these things out together.

The second reason you'll want to understand that listening can be draining is so you can monitor yourself in conversations. If a person is sitting there listening to you, don't take it for granted. After several minutes, ask them for their perspective on your issue or ask them about themselves. If you've got to talk about something that will require more time, say in advance, "I've had a lot going on, and this might take 15 or 20 minutes to say it all. Would you have the time and energy to hear me out?" It's all about respecting their energy and not taking their listening for granted. In the communication world, there's so much talk about just listening without trying to fix the problem. There's value in that. We all need and want to be heard. The part that doesn't get discussed enough is that it's an act of service to listen to someone, as energy and effort go into it. Therefore, be cognizant of both sides of the coin. If someone doesn't want advice and they want you to just listen, you can do that for them. If you're the one speaking, be respectful of the person doing the listening by sticking to the relevant subject matter and having in mind exactly what you want to get off your chest.

Some people have difficulty understanding what it is they actually need to get off their chest. When this happens, you might share every detail of a story, from the clothes the people were wearing, how the weather was that day, to the carpets in the building having been freshly cleaned. Remember, listening requires energy, so details unrelated to your main issue put your listener in a difficult position.

If Jim said something off-putting at work today and you're feeling angry and anxious about his comment, it may not be necessary to know that Jim's beard isn't well-trimmed, his shoes never match his outfits, and the director of a different department was out sick that day.

Ask yourself, "What's the crux of what I want to get off my chest? What's the issue that's really weighing on me?" Well, Jim's untrimmed beard doesn't look great, but without his off-putting comment, he'd just be a regular guy with a messy beard. And his shoes that never match? Again, he'd be a regular guy whose outfit doesn't match just like the millions of other guys whose outfits don't match. How about the director of another department being out? You've only talked to that director once. Plus, they'd have exactly zero to do with your issue, even if you filed a complaint. How about your feelings of anger and anxiety? Hey, now you're getting somewhere!

Your feelings about what Jim said to you are the crux of the issue. You can now filter out everything that isn't related to your feelings. You can say, "Jim said ABC and XYZ to me at work today. I feel really mad about that. I think I'm mad about it because it reminds me of how my dad used to talk to me as a kid. I just wanted to yell at Jim in that moment. As a kid, I couldn't stand up for myself against my dad, and part of me wants to really let Jim have it!"

Since you've expressed your emotions, you can return to work and handle the situation professionally with Jim. You might let it slide but keep your radar up. If it happens two more times, you'll say something to Jim. If it happens again after that, you'll file a report or do everything in your power to relocate your desk.

The skill of stripping down what you want to say to the heart of the matter can be great for your partnership. It relieves your partner of having to hear what could be described as meaningless details while allowing you to express the core of what's weighing on you. Much deeper communication takes place in less time.

There's a lot of talk about people who won't or can't listen. That's for good reason because it can be crazy-making to try and have a conversation with someone who won't listen and only thinks about what they want to say next. However, the issue of listening energy and being cognizant of how much time and energy you're asking of the person listening to you is important, too, and rarely talked about. Don't misread this message. It isn't meant to say you should never let someone be a listener for you or be a listener for someone else. This is about being aware of asking the other person questions and letting them share about their lives if you do most of the talking or ensuring you take time to insert yourself into the conversation if you usually do most of the listening. If you have an issue that will take significant time, simply asking the person in advance if they have the time and energy to hear you out will go a long way.

~

If you're not great at listening, how can you become good at it? It would be helpful to first look at why you're not good at listening. As a therapist and human being, I've encountered lots of people who can't or won't listen. Except for a disability being involved, there's only one reason a person can't or won't listen: What they're saying in their own mind is more interesting or important to them than what the other person is saying.

Regarding basic conversation, none of our thoughts are all that important other than to us. I've always been interested in reading and learning about military special forces like Navy SEALs and Delta Force, and had a conversation with someone about that topic a few days ago. I was sharing what I knew about the raid on bin Laden. I talked about how one helicopter went down and how the neighborhood was woken up by the noise, causing crowds of people to converge on the compound. The person I was talking with shared about how tough the Navy SEALs are and about his friend who was a sharpshooter or marksman— neither of us knew the difference. I could tell that neither of us cared much about what the other was saying. I was sharing things about a topic I was interested in, Navy SEALs, and he was sharing things about a topic he liked, shooting. It was a nice little conversation but probably not all that important to either of us in the grand scheme of things.

Something to remember when listening is that people generally care far less about your thoughts and far more about having a sense of being heard. Do you want to form a connection with someone? Ask them about their life. What are you genuinely interested in knowing about them? Don't do this from a stance of being nosy but from one of genuine interest. A few questions you can ask that'll help you develop a connection are:

How do you like your job?

What do you really want to do? Are you doing it? What's holding you back?

What were your favorite movies as a kid?

Can you say more about what you meant by . . .

What were your parents like when you were growing up?

Where would you want to visit in the world?

What challenges are you dealing with right now in life?

How did you handle [X]? I'm dealing with/going through [X] right now, so that's why I'm asking. What was your experience of it?

What are you having fun with or what's going well right now?

What are the best books you've read lately or in the last several years?

If you can ask people fun, engaging, or interesting questions about themselves, they'll have a blast answering. Make sure the questions don't cross the line in terms of being nosy or too personal (of course, the closer you are with someone, the more personal you can get). As a general guideline, people love talking about their lives, what they're up to, what their challenges are, what they've learned, what they know, and what their dreams are.

The other factor in becoming an excellent listener is that you'll respond more effectively if you truly hear what your partner has to say. If you're half listening, only catching a few words here and there because you're thinking about what you want to say, your response will be half appropriate, half effective, and half interesting. Your partner will have a sense that you kind of understand, but not fully. Many people perceive themselves as knowing more than most other people. You could know more than others all you want, but nobody else will grasp how much you know if your listening skills aren't developed. You might know a lot, but they won't care because your responses will have little to do with the thoughts and feelings they shared. If you want others to view you as knowing a lot, listen closely and deeply to what they say before responding. Your response will be more on point for them, and they will view you as someone who "gets it."

~

People value responding quickly during conversations. That's okay, but it can lead to a lack of connection. A pause between responses isn't necessarily a sign of not knowing what to say next. It's a sign of assimilating what the other person said before responding. My therapist often takes a long time to respond after I've shared something, but it always brings me deeper into understanding myself.

To listen well, there needs to be more space in conversations. Normalize a period of silence for you and your partner to consider how you'd like to respond to what the other has said. If you're attached to responding immediately, then you'll have no other option but to be thinking about your response while the other person is still speaking. If there's silence between each person speaking, you can fully listen while they speak and then fully focus on your response. Stop viewing silence as "awkward" and begin viewing it as an important aspect of deeply connected conversations.

~

You don't automatically have to understand everything the other person says to be an effective listener. That's the magic of it. If your partner says something and you're not understanding what they mean or what they're getting at, it's okay. You can still be a top-notch listener by utilizing clarifying questions.

Relationship Skill #9
Ask Clarifying Questions

Instead of going with your initial interpretation of a situation, ask clarifying questions.

Clarifying questions get their own chapter because the skill has two uses. The first use is as a listening skill. The second use is to effectively sort out your relationship.

When being in the role of the listener in your partnership—and hopefully, you and your partner have a fairly even exchange of being the listener and talker—clarifying questions can do wonders. Ask a clarifying question when you don't understand what your partner is saying or attempting to communicate.

Them: "I don't know about chicken again tonight. We've had it a lot lately."

You: "God, you're picky. If you don't like my cooking, just say so."

The above response was knee-jerk in nature. Let's try again.

Them: "I don't know about chicken again tonight. We've had it a lot lately."

You: "Are you saying you want anything but chicken, or is there something specific you want?" Or "Chicken is really easy for me to make. That's why I make it. Would you rather help me make something else or just stick with chicken? I'm willing to make chicken myself because it's simple. But for something else, I'd ask for your help."

Healthy communication does not mean you have to always do whatever your partner requests. They don't want chicken? No problem. But you still get to protect your time and energy by requesting help.

When communicating, it can be challenging to get across exactly what you want to say in the first statement of a discussion. That's why clarifying questions are magical. They relieve you of having to automatically understand what's being said while also leaving your partner with a sense that you're asking relevant questions to understand.

Listening well isn't just about sitting quietly and waiting for the person to run out of words. Listening well involves asking questions that, when answered, will deepen your understanding of what the other person is attempting to say. Don't think of listening as just sitting there and nodding your head. Think of listening as digging for a better understanding of the other person.

~

Clarifying questions can help you sort through relationship issues. Based on my work with couples, I've concluded that it would be very helpful if every couple agreed to be asked clarifying questions by their partner. Before moving ahead, know a couple of issues can come up when asking your partner clarifying questions.

The second most common issue (we'll get to the first most common issue in a minute) is that people are so attached to their self-image that they're not open to being asked questions. People can become deathly offended if someone else thinks they have anything but saintly motives and divinely pure intentions. Of course, this is a defense mechanism and not based on reality, but it exemplifies how strongly people are attached to their self-image. Around the year 2012, I was trying out online dating. I'd been talking to someone, and sparks were in the air. She was into sports like me; we had similar worldviews and found one another attractive. Yes, sparky indeed. I wish I could remember what it was specifically about, but I asked her a question she didn't like. I can't remember the question, but I remember her answer: "How could you ask that? You don't know me at all." When you're strongly attached to your self-image, questions can be threatening. It's unsettling to find out your partner doesn't necessarily see you how you see yourself. It's helpful to be curious about how your partner sees you, but it takes guts. You must have a sense of self-confidence to be open to hearing exactly how your partner perceives you. Where you see strength in yourself, they might see instability. Where you see bravery, they might see fear. Where you see masculinity, they might see compensatory behavior. Where you see kindness, they might see people pleasing. Once again, this brings you back to whether you'd rather face honest challenges in your relationship right now or future challenges resulting from a lack of open communication.

Regarding how you and your partner see one another, agree to view it all as projection. You might say, "I see myself as kind, but maybe it's actually about my need to be validated." Or, "I see myself as tough and strong, but it could be a way to cover up the shame and powerlessness I felt as a young boy." Everything *is* projection anyways, and the sooner you can accept that about your self-image, the more deeply connected and interesting your partnership can become. When you're the one sharing how you see your partner, say, "This is how I see it. I'm not claiming it to be absolute truth. I'm just saying that this is how I perceive you in this particular area."

Why all this talk about how you perceive one another? When you ask clarifying questions, it might let on that you're not seeing your partner in the most ego-inflating light. For example, if you ask, "What did you mean by what you just said?" and they respond, "Why are you asking?" you'll then say, "Because it seemed like a put-down." If your partner is strongly attached to their self-image, they might say, "How dare you think I would ever put you down. That's just insulting." But if your partner is open and curious, they might say, "Interesting. Here's why I said that and how I meant it." If your partner is open and really into their inner healing journey, they might say, "Yes, I did mean that as a put-down. I owe you an apology." Or, if they give a reasonable, understandable explanation for why they said what they did, you might say, "I misinterpreted what you said there. I'm sorry for thinking the worst." And that brings us to the number one most common issue when asking clarifying questions.

The most common problem with using clarifying questions is that people believe their interpretations of events, comments, and motivations. "That was a put-down," you might say. "I know it was. You did that on purpose to make me feel bad." Maybe, maybe not. Take a moment to consider how likely you are to believe your first interpretation of events.

The beauty of clarifying questions is they relieve you of needing to be attached to your initial interpretation. You get to ask questions like, "Are you angry?" "What did you mean by that?" or "Why did you use that tone of voice when you said that?" Clarifying questions allow you to find out what's really going on.

When you were growing up, you probably had to interpret events to keep yourself safe. *Dad's body language is becoming aggressive. I'll go to my room and be quiet, so I'm out of the way when things get crazy.* Or, *Mom's walking back and forth around the house quickly and seems stressed. The last time she did that, I got screamed at. I'll try to keep out of the way.*

Quickly interpreting events served you well as a child because it kept you out of harm's way, whether the harm was emotional or physical. With an adult partnership, sticking with your initial interpretation of events may hold you back from deeper intimacy. The invitation here is to be curious rather than jumping to conclusions.

Recall that earlier in the book, there was a chapter on seeking truth at all costs. Agreeing to ask one another clarifying questions only works if both parties are on board. You both must agree to:

A. Set aside your initial judgments and interpretations.

B. Be willing to ask and be asked questions that may not always paint you or your partner in an ego-bolstering light.

C. Be willing to answer in a way that values truth at all costs above self-image or winning.

Some people simply won't be capable of utilizing clarifying questions in their partnership because they're still at a point where shame is too strong. To be wrong or to have committed a hurtful act is too much to bear, and shame takes over. This prevents a person from seeking truth. Instead, they're seeking self-protection or protection of self-image. Or if shame doesn't take over, a strong defensiveness takes over. People with a strong defensiveness have difficulty acknowledging wrongdoing and apologizing. They may also lie to avoid the emotional consequences of their actions. When someone is overtaken by shame or has a barricade of defensiveness around them, clarifying questions won't be useful. This is why the first relationship skill in this book is Seek Truth at All Costs. Without it, many of the other skills are useless. This isn't about just applying a special tone of voice or wording something in the right way to get the response you're hoping for out of your partner. It's about truly getting down to the bottom of things.

Set aside your initial judgments and interpretations.
Your interpretation of events is alluring. After all, it's *yours*. It's happening in your head and in your body. It's so true . . . for you.

We were visiting my parents for the holidays, and I had bought groceries. I brought the bags into the kitchen and started unloading them. I put everything that would go in the refrigerator into one bag and everything that would go in the cupboard into another bag. The kitchen at my parents' house is long and narrow, like a hallway. It's easier to load all the perishables into one bag and then put them away all at once as opposed to walking back and forth. I finished putting away the perishables bag, then went back to the kitchen table to get the bag of food items that would go in the cupboard. Except, everything was spread out on the table, not in a bag.

My mom was standing there, and I said, "Hey, I put those in that bag so I could carry them all at once to the cupboard."

She said, "Oh, sorry for taking them out. I'll put them back for you."

False. She did not say that.

She said, "This is how they were. They weren't in a bag."

I paused for a moment and realized I had *thought* about putting them into a bag but hadn't actually done so. I said, "I'm sorry, I thought I loaded them into a bag but realize I never did."

When it comes to interpreting events, our minds are capable of anything. It's much wiser to be willing to set aside our interpretations to discover what's true than to be attached to what we initially think. You may discover your initial interpretation to be accurate or like me in the instance above, you might discover your mind jumped to a conclusion based on only inner perception but not external reality.

Be willing to ask and be asked questions that may not always paint you or your partner in an ego-bolstering light.
Generally, people don't want to be asked difficult questions. However, it can be immensely helpful to understand where your partner's mind was when they said or did a certain action.

A couple I worked with had difficulty sorting out an issue. While the husband was away on a business trip, the wife had gone to her bowling league. Pictures surfaced on social media of the wife sitting closely with a man at the bowling venue, as sometimes businesses will take photos during events for promotional purposes. They were laughing and having a good time together, and the wife admitted to the husband that things became flirtatious.

The wife stated that the flirting went too far, but there was no kissing or sexual contact. Since that was her experience of the situation, she wanted it to be done and over with. The husband had additional questions, as the experience brought up trust issues within their partnership. From this point forward, the wife's chief complaint in therapy was that her husband wouldn't stop asking her questions about what happened at the bowling alley.

The issue with the wife was she felt immense shame for what had happened. Because her shame was so intense, she couldn't bear to discuss the subject with her husband. She defended against her shame by turning it around on him and telling him he's asking too many questions and needs to get over it because nothing physical happened.

To sort out issues and create trust in a relationship, we need to be willing to acknowledge the pain our actions cause. That's difficult. Acknowledging how your words or actions affected your partner can be tremendously painful. I suspect that if the wife could understand the pain and confusion created by her actions, she would have been more open to answering questions from her partner.

When dealing with immense shame, the options aren't plentiful. They consist of either defending against the shame or breaking down. Here, the wife was defending against the shame of how she felt about what she did. The other option would have been to break down into tears over the pain it caused.

Many relationships could be repaired if people could break down into heartfelt tears over the pain they caused rather than defend themselves. People don't do this because they're stuck in the old belief that showing your pain leads to being abused or taken advantage of by a parent, caregiver, or peer. In partnerships, your significant other *needs* to see that you feel utter agony over the pain you created. If you don't feel much pain or experience much regret over the wrongdoing, how are they to trust you again? Is it significant to you that you caused pain, or insignificant? Your partner wants you to show one way or the other so they understand where you stand. They may assume you aren't experiencing remorse if you're defensive or emotionally stone-faced. Saying, "Oh, yeah, oops, sorry about that. Okay, let's move on and drop it," doesn't inspire trust and a desire to reconnect.

This isn't saying you have to get down on your knees and beg. It's saying that defending against the agony you feel over the pain you've caused isn't doing your relationship any favors. It could be beneficial to shed tears, if they're authentic, over what you did.

~

When being the one who's asking clarifying questions, you've got to be honest and direct. What's weighing on your mind about the situation? What's eating at you?

It could help to discuss your feelings with a therapist or coach first, as most issues within a relationship have two parts: the part that's truly about the here and now of your relationship and the part that reminds you of old experiences from your

to be asked the questions. It can be challenging being the one asking and being the one who's being asked, but getting down to the bottom of the issue rather than avoiding it is the only way to create something workable moving forward.

Relationship Skill #10
Don't Immediately Blame Your Partner

Instead of immediately blaming your partner, examine your projections.

I've mentioned my mentor, Ron, throughout many of my books. Another significant piece of wisdom he passed along is that if you don't work through your old issues pertaining to your parents or caregivers, you'll project them onto your partner.

A client was considering asking a woman he was dating to marry him. This client had done significant inner healing work on himself. During 10 years, he had done shadow work, emotional processing and expression work, worked through his parental wounds, and attended many workshops. The woman he was dating was very interested in doing the inner work herself but had limited experience with it.

This client explained that his girlfriend had some unresolved issues involving her father. Serious issues. He was an aggressive man who tried to control her life. This was true when she was a child and still true as she was on the precipice of turning 30. In discussing engagement and marriage, I explained to this client that if she hasn't done her inner work around her father, she would project her issues with him onto him (my client). I wasn't dissuading or persuading him to marry her; I was laying out what he could expect so he could decide for himself.

Ultimately, they got married and ran into issues early on. Within weeks—not even a month—of getting married, my client explained that something had shifted. His formerly happy, fun fiancé had become withdrawn and rather serious about everything. The openness between them had dissolved. To be clear, it hadn't dissolved from him to her, but it had dissolved from her to him. It was clear what was happening.

Now that they were living together (they didn't live together before getting married), my client had become a significant male relationship in his partner's life. In dating and engagement, it isn't so serious, as walking away can be done more easily and simply. Such a significant relationship with a male brought up his wife's programming. In her first and most significant relationship with a male (her father), she hid away as much as possible, remaining quiet and withdrawn to avoid his aggression and controlling behavior. When they started living under the same roof, the old programming was activated, and she was interacting with my client the same way she interacted with her father. Except, there was no real danger with my client, as he knew how to communicate and validate perspectives and emotions. His wife saw danger from the eyes in her own head, and that's how projection works.

People often think projection means seeing things that aren't there. This isn't true. It's not whether what you're seeing is there, it's a question of where what you're seeing is located. Is it in the external world or is it in your psyche? With projection, it's in your psyche.

What my client's partner was seeing was there, indeed. However, she was confused about where it was located. I wish I could say they worked the issue out over a few months. Unfortunately, his partner had undergone such long-term and intense trauma from her father that, three years later, they're still sorting it out. They're having a difficult time in their marriage, even having discussed separating. Three years of withdrawing and not communicating will harm a relationship in the same way that three years of name-calling and verbal abuse will harm it. The mode is different, but the lack of connection created by the behavior is the same.

When you have unresolved issues, your psyche ~~insists~~ demands that they be acknowledged, addressed, and healed. This demand is so strong that your psyche will cause you to see your inner issues in outer situations. In the case of my client above, his partner was seeing him as she saw her father, even though he wasn't the same as her father. The issues within her psyche demanded acknowledgment. If you don't acknowledge a trauma or emotional wound from your past, your psyche will cause you to see that issue anywhere and everywhere: In your partner, in your children, in your boss or coworkers, at the gym, online (think of all the arguments online based on simple misinterpretations), and so on.

Our conscious minds think the most important things in life are happiness, security, money, nice cars, expensive toys, nice houses, presenting a good body, and being admired by others. The psyche begs to differ. To the psyche, the most important things in life are purpose, meaning, healing, psychological development, and acting in alignment with your deepest self. When fixated on the goals of the ego, it might not cross your mind that the issues you're having with your partner could represent an old emotional wound or trauma you haven't addressed, as with my client and his spouse.

This can become tricky because almost *anybody* can remind us of almost *anybody else*. For example, my client reminded his partner of her father just by being a man. As a personal example, my father displayed anger and rage when I was growing up through yelling and slamming doors. He was a strong man with a deep, loud voice. I feared him. Fast forward many years to a retreat I attended as a young adult. There was a man there wearing a red and black flannel shirt, the same design my father often wore. I was immediately and automatically threatened by this man, judging he was mean, angry, and emotionally dangerous. He had none of those qualities. He was friendly, kind, and thoughtful. As you can see, what I saw was there. I wasn't imagining things. However, I needed to sort out where what I was seeing was located. I was incorrect to think it was in the man wearing the red and black flannel. To honor my psyche and move toward inner healing, I had to look within myself for the qualities I saw in the man. In doing so, I could begin addressing the effects being raised in an environment of rage had on my worldviews, self-perceptions, and general life experiences.

Almost anybody can remind us of anybody else. That we're being "re-minded" of something is proof it's an unresolved psychological issue within our own minds. That me seeing a man in a red and black flannel re-minded me to be scared, anxious, and on guard was proof there was an unresolved issue within me.

A quick environmental safety check is necessary when we are reminded of danger. Are you physically safe? Could a violent situation take place? If the man in the red and black flannel was showing signs of insanity or violence, I would have been wise to have left. But he was doing nothing other than existing as a human who wore that shirt to the retreat. Is that cause to withdraw, run, defend, fight, or freeze? Of course not. Similarly, if my client's partner had done an environmental safety check, she may have seen there was not only no danger present, but there were many opportunities for emotional safety and connection. The issue was that her trauma from her father was so terrifying that it was too scary to peek out of her shell for a moment to see if the danger was still there. That's not to blame her for responding negatively to her trauma, as she didn't choose to be hurt by her father and subsequently too scared to engage with her husband. With that said, for the pattern to change, a person must be willing to let go of old defense mechanisms for at least a few seconds to try something new and different. A traumatized person will do this when they're ready and not when their partner or anyone else wants them to, and therein lies the immense challenge in such situations. Trauma defense mechanisms aren't activated with intent to purposefully harm the other partner, and most partners are understanding due to that fact. With that said, the defense mechanisms still cause harm to the relationship, whether purposeful or not. If someone accidentally hits you with their car, damage was caused, whether intentional or unintentional. While most people offer understanding to their partners who are dealing with trauma, they're still only human and can offer only so much. If the trauma patterns don't change, the supporting partner will eventually become burned out and exhausted. Sometimes, they might want separation. Not out of blame or criticism but out of the fact that no connection is happening due to the trauma defense mechanisms of withdrawal or lashing out constantly being in the picture. Most commonly, a burned-out supporting partner will leave emotionally and not literally.

Often, the traumatized partner wants to communicate, but it's too scary to do so. In one case, a man said to his partner, "I'm just not ready to communicate." That's honest and fair. However, it also puts his partner in a sticky situation. Remember, both partners are only human. No matter how virtuous, the one who wants to communicate will have a finite capacity to support and wait for the uncommunicative partner to open up. In such cases, there must be mutual dedication. The one ready to communicate must be dedicated to supporting and understanding their partner's challenges. The one who isn't ready to communicate must be dedicated to seeking safe environments (therapy, therapy group, 12-step groups, workshops, mentors) that will lead them to open up. Without mutual dedication, starting today, not tomorrow, one of the two partners will eventually burn out and leave the relationship, either literally or emotionally.

Issues with your partner will remind you of the past occasionally. It's helpful to ask yourself whether it's an ongoing problem or a minor situation. If someone withdraws from a tough conversation one time but comes back to talk the next day and never does it again, that's not a huge problem. If they withdraw from every challenging conversation, that's an enormous problem that must be addressed. If someone slips up and calls you a name once but never does it again, that's not a huge problem. If they're constantly name-calling, that needs to be addressed. Since triggers are so powerful, assessing whether something is a projection or a true relationship problem can be difficult. Assess not only how you feel but the objective facts of how this issue has or has not shown up in the relationship. Avoid immediately blaming your partner, especially in topics that aren't clear-cut. Drinking, driving, and getting a DUI is clear-cut, as is your partner punching you in the face. Your partner making an off-putting comment here and there isn't clear-cut. It will require self-reflection on your part (What about this is triggering me? Is an old wound involved?). It will require discussion with your partner and lots of clarifying questions.

On the flipside, your partner may be triggered by you. This will happen, too. A friend was telling me about his partner one day, explaining that her father was an addict. Her father was no longer using, but used often when she was growing up. Apparently, one day, my friend had said something that reminded his partner of her addict father, and she told him so. When my friend came to me, he was offended that anything he could do would remind her of her father. After all, he'd never abused drugs.

I explained to my friend that it's okay to have micro-moments when you remind your partner of a significant person who was extremely negative in their lives. It's not only okay, but it's bound to happen. I explained that it doesn't mean he's like her father at every moment and in all cases. It simply means there was a moment when a similarity came up, a "re-minder." In a healthy partnership, you can accept that occasionally your partner will see something in you that reminds them of someone negative from their past. It's only momentary. This isn't about your entire personhood, it's about one small moment. Additionally, in a healthy relationship, your partner can see this isn't who you are; it was just something momentary. In this example, it doesn't mean my friend was like his partner's father. If she's healthy and aware, she'll be able to see that this was but a moment in time. They can talk about it, validate where each person is coming from, apologize and make up where needed, find a mutually agreeable way to move forward, and be better off in their relationship. This won't work if one or both partners are either unaccepting that the other could see something negative in them or unable to see it as a moment in time over a long-term definition of who the person is.

Projection is powerful, and there's no escaping it. There's only acknowledging it and working with it. Remember: you project because there's something unresolved in your psyche. Whenever you have a problem with your partner, first check in with yourself, asking, "Is this reminding me of an old experience?" If it is, that doesn't necessarily mean you don't address it with your partner. It means you do the emotional processing work within yourself in addition to addressing it with your partner.

Back to the story of my client and his wife from the beginning of this chapter. Fortunately, she's been working through her emotions about her father as well as speaking up more in the relationship. For the relationship to thrive, she'll have to continue expressing herself. If one person isn't expressing themselves in a relationship, that's not a relationship. If you're not expressing who you are to your partner, then there's nothing for your partner to connect with. At best, the relationship can be functional or transactional, helping one another with chores and duties. At worst, you'll be utterly miserable because you want to share who you are and experience who someone else is, but it won't be possible when withdrawal is happening.

If my client's partner continues expressing herself, the relationship can develop into something strong. However, I'm also aware of how powerful these old wounds and traumas can be. I wouldn't be surprised if my client reported that his partner has gone back into withdrawal and a discontinuation of sharing what's true for her. By remaining vigilant and having a support system (groups, meetings, therapy, people she can call), she can make self-expression within the relationship a natural part of her life. Without a support system in place, it can be all too easy for her to fall back into the old pattern. For them, time will tell. For yourself, what do you choose?

Relationship Skill #11
Happy Relationships Require More than Financial Provision

Instead of expecting your partner to be happy based solely on financial provision, develop a true connection.

Finances are important. There's a lot to be said for a person who supports their family financially. It provides a place to live, warmth and shelter from rain, snow, wind, cold, animals, and insects. The living space most often also includes a water system for drinking and taking nice, warm showers. It's truly a life-changing thing to have shelter. Most of us have always had shelter, so we take it for granted. For a moment, imagine living out in the woods without a warm, dry area and no water supply. Imagine being exposed to any animal or insect that comes your way—coyotes, skunks, mosquitos, ticks. A financial living also provides food. Food keeps your brain, heart, muscles, and other vital body systems running properly. Without food, you'd wither away. Food also gives pleasure. It's nice to enjoy a good meal, dessert, or snack at the table in a dry living space. Imagine if your belly was always grumbling and gargling because of hunger. When someone provides a living for their family, it's truly no small thing, and that's easy to see when you imagine life without financial provision.

Yet . . .

As vitally important as a financial living is, it's not enough to create a connected, fulfilling relationship with your partner. There are two sides to this issue. Both are important, and both need to be addressed. I've often had clients say something like, "I work hard. Every day, I get up at 5:00 am and go to work. I provide a house and lots of other nice things. My spouse doesn't work. My spouse can do whatever they want all day long. Yet, they complain about our relationship and get angry and frustrated with me."

With the partner who is the one providing the living, two issues often come up in therapy. One issue is that they want to be appreciated. This is reasonable and necessary. Without appreciation, it's unlikely a relationship will thrive. If one partner is providing a living and the other partner never expresses appreciation, it's as if the time, energy, and effort given toward making a living isn't valued by the other partner. Whether you're dedicating your life to making a living for your family or dedicating it to raising well-adjusted, happy, healthy children, everyone wants their efforts acknowledged and appreciated.

The second issue that often comes up is that they want their partner to have no complaints because they're the ones making a living, and their partner gets to do whatever they please all day. While appreciation for this is appropriate and necessary, having no complaints is only a fantasy and unreasonable. Giving someone the financial means to spend their days as they wish or to remain at home raising the children (if they want to do that) does not automatically equal a connected relationship. Only one thing leads to a connected relationship.

Providing someone a nice house, car, and freedom to do what they wish with their time doesn't create a deep connection between two people. It's a reason for them to be appreciative, absolutely, but it won't necessarily create emotional bonds.

Emotional bonds are formed through mutually opening up to one another and caring about one another. For example, if your partner says, "I feel angry and hurt when you call me that name," this is a chance for true connection to form. If you wave your hand and storm off or say, "Oh yeah? Well, I feel angry when you . . ." you'll have missed an opportunity to connect. Now your partner has to disconnect from you more because they can't discuss their feelings with you without being blown off or further criticized. Or if they don't disconnect, they'll be trying to force themselves to stay in connection despite having a sense of not being cared about, and that's an uphill, losing battle. Connection is formed when you each share the things that truly matter to you, and then you each care about what truly matters to the other person.

In the example above, a useful response would be, "You're right; it was wrong of me to call you that name. I let my anger and frustration get out of hand there, and that's not okay. I'm sorry." Had you responded that way, your partner's defenses could drop because they would have a sense that you care about what matters to them, which, in this case, is how their emotions felt when they were called the name. No amount of money could ever make up for mutually caring about one another.

This same concept applies to things that bring joy, fulfillment, and happiness. It's important to care about your partner's feelings when they're hurt, sad, angry, etc. It's also important to care when they're happy and fulfilled or want to pursue things that are meaningful to them. For example, maybe your partner is writing a book. This has been a lifelong dream for them. Are you happy they're fulfilling their dream, or are you jealous, or worse, indifferent? Emotional connection forms when you show care and enthusiasm about your partner's fulfillment and satisfaction.

~

We've touched on how providing a living isn't enough to form a connected partnership. On the flip side of that, it's also problematic if you take your partner's financial provision for granted. While material things can't provide ultimate fulfillment, they're still nice to have. If you stay at home with the kids or manage the household, you might stop every now and then and think how nice it is to have a roof over your head. Every now and then, once a month, remember to express your appreciation to your partner. You can say, "I like our home so much. Thank you for working to provide for it." Put it in your own words.

If your partner struggles to be emotionally available, you expressing appreciation doesn't excuse them from the need to emotionally heal and become more available. You express appreciation because you appreciate the things you have. Then you continue to bring up the issues within the relationship. You can explain that your appreciation of their hard work doesn't mean you don't also want a deeper connection.

Additionally, another functional matter is that it's important to be aware of your life agreements. For example, the agreement may be that you both work and contribute to the finances. Or the agreement may be that one of you works while the other manages the home and does most of what's needed for the kids. Whatever your agreement is, make it conscious—avoid falling into something with no discussion.

In one case, the agreement may be that one of you works while the other does everything for the household. This could include yard maintenance, hiring contractors for repairs when needed, paying the bills, keeping the home clean, doing the laundry, cooking, and so forth. In another case, children may be involved. If this is your situation, your agreement may require a more in-depth discussion. Children require lots of evening drives for sports, extracurriculars, friend meetups, and other activities. They also require managing their food and medical needs. Extra laundry, extra cleaning, extra planning. I've heard many cases where the partner who works assumes that's their only responsibility. They've never had a discussion with their partner about distribution of other needs like errands and household chores. The time and energy it takes to raise kids often goes unacknowledged. There's a difference between physical energy, which is often what working a job requires, and emotional energy, which raising children requires. They're different types of energy, but energy, nonetheless. In your partnership, it's important to converse about your experiences working a job, running the household, and raising children. How drained are each of you? Where and how do you need support? You may discover that neither of you has ever expressed what daily life is like. You might find your partner is burned out from their job, and they secretly hate it. It eats away at their soul every day, but they haven't expressed this to you out of not wanting to bother you with it. Or you might find your partner is hanging on by a thread emotionally each day when it comes to raising the kids. They have a sense of being all alone and needing support but haven't mentioned this to you out of not wanting to bother you with their stress. Have an open conversation and commit to however long it takes to find mutually supportive ways forward. Mutually care about what's important to your partner. It could take multiple conversations over weeks or months. Stick with it, and don't fall back into the old patterns that haven't worked for you. Working *toward* something together, even if you don't find answers immediately, is always better than having a sense of being *stuck* in a miserable situation without your partner's support. Again, keep the conversation going until you arrive at mutually agreeable ways forward.

To summarize, if you provide financially for your family, that's truly an act of love. However, if you're expecting financial provision to equal ultimate satisfaction for your partner, you will be severely disappointed. You'll need to practice expressing the things that deeply matter to you. You must also practice caring about the things that deeply matter to your partner.

Relationship Skill #12
Less Talk, More Action

Instead of discussing your relationship issues ad infinitum, take action.

Talking with your partner is necessary. You've got to communicate to sort out and organize the day-to-day and long-term decisions. Talking can also be a form of enjoyment and pleasure when it's about fun, light topics or topics of interest that bear no immediate impact on your lives. However, when working through relationship issues, sometimes talking isn't enough.

A client, Jessica, came with an issue about her husband, Chris. She said he wasn't following through on their discussions. She described that they lived several hours apart when they first met. They decided to get married, and since she was renting and he owned a house, they decided they would live in his house for a year, sell it, and then move. They came to this decision in advance of getting married because Jessica wasn't interested in living where Chris was from over the long term, but she was willing to live there for a year while they sorted out their plans to relocate to an area they both liked. Chris agreed to this.

But once they were already married and she had moved her life several hours away to his town, Chris then became unwilling to discuss moving. Every time Jessica brought it up, Chris would evade the subject. This pattern didn't start and end with the moving situation. Many agreements they made about their lives or relationship weren't followed through on. Jessica asked Chris if he would share his feelings about their relationship, like, for example, if he was upset with her about something. He agreed. When the time came, he would quietly burn up inside without telling her he was upset with her.

By the time Jessica came to me, there had been agreements made and not followed through on in several areas of their relationship, leading to corrosion of trust. Plus, Jessica was still living in his town after a few years of marriage, where she was still unhappy. The pattern was that they would make an agreement about their lives together, Chris wouldn't follow through on the agreement, Jessica would bring it up several weeks later, Chris would apologize, and then Chris would again not follow through on the agreement even after apologizing.

After some digging into Chris's past, Jessica discovered that conversations about life only happened in his household growing up beneath the iron fist of his mother. There were no conversations involving two people seeking mutually agreeable ways to move forward. It was a dictatorship. Chris learned to nod his head in agreement to cope because that ended the interaction more quickly. His mother's attention would soon be diverted to either his father or siblings, thus getting him off the hook of actually having to do whatever his mother was demanding. The issue is that Jessica wasn't trying to rule over Chris. She was trying to build a life with him where they could both be reasonably satisfied. For Jessica, being reasonably satisfied meant relocating to an area they both liked. It also meant checking in with one another and sharing feelings when either partner was upset with the other one.

Jessica and Chris would engage in long conversations about their issues. She explained that talking felt good, but it never resulted in any change. Chris still wasn't following through on their agreements. Jessica wanted action, not more talk.

Eventually, Jessica took it upon herself to move, renting a place in an area she liked. She planned to rent for a year, and if Chris wasn't willing to move, she would seek a permanent place for herself. She explained that she realized no number of conversations would lead to change, and her options were to either accept living in Chris's town or move. If he followed up on his original agreement, great. If he didn't, she would accept the dissolution of their partnership. As it turned out, Chris was willing to recognize that he had made an agreement about moving with Jessica. He prepared his house for sale, and they found a new place.

The relationship skill here is to not force your partner to choose between accepting something they hate (e.g., Jessica living in a town she didn't like) and taking extreme action (e.g., Jessica moving on her own without her partner). Chris didn't wake up until Jessica took the extreme action of moving without him. Such extreme actions are stressful on each individual involved, but especially on the one in the position of their partner not following through on agreements. You can save yourself and your relationship much grief by following through on your and your partner's discussions. If you agree on something, let your words be enough to inspire you to follow through. Don't wait until your partner brings it up again. Let your yes mean yes, and your no mean no. If you're not on board with a plan of action, don't agree to it. Continue the discussion until you arrive at a mutually agreeable way forward. Once you agree on something, be proactive in following through.

Additionally, an aspect of this skill involves acting on one another's behalf. With long-term relationships, it's easy to settle into a comfort zone. Chris was comfortable remaining where he lived. It would have required an activation of energy for him to keep his word to Jessica. Because she moved to his town, he was comfortable with her daily presence. With that security in place, he became complacent because his relationship needs were met. He lost sight of how important it was for him to gather the inner resources and energy to act on Jessica's behalf and put in the effort to move someplace they both were reasonably happy with.

Regarding relationships, one person being comfortable doesn't equal a happy relationship—it equals one person's comfort. Here, Chris's comfort came at the expense of the integrity of the relationship. It would have been uncomfortable for him to put in the effort to move—and no doubt moving requires lots of energy—but the discomfort would have been temporary. In keeping his word to Jessica, the relationship would have maintained its well-being, and both individuals within the partnership would have eventually settled into the new area. Because Jessica had to take such extreme action for Christ to keep his word, will she ever feel the same about him again, or will the size of the scar be too big to manage?

Don't lose sight of there being two people in a partnership. If one partner is terribly unhappy, it will inevitably lead to major relationship issues. Therefore, within reason, act on behalf of your partner and insist your partner do the same. If it's not mutual, the only one acting on the other's behalf will eventually pull away, or if they don't pull away, they'll become so exhausted that they won't have any presence to give to the relationship, so it'll be as if they've pulled away. Don't solely *take* from your relationship. Likewise, don't solely *give* to your relationship. Seek a balance of having your needs met and acting on behalf of your partner to meet their needs.

~

Is there an issue you've been saying you'll act on but haven't? Each day that goes by without acting on something you said you would take action on eats away at trust little by little. As the saying goes, the way you eat an elephant is one bite at a time. Eventually, whether it's in a few months, a year, or a few years, the entire elephant will have been eaten, leaving little or no trust between you and your partner.

If there's an issue at hand and you know you need to seek help or pursue change, don't take your partner for granted. As a more extreme example, it can be easy for an alcoholic to ask for more time to work through their issue, but it's much harder on the person who's granting more time. Don't put your partner in a position of having to grant you more time, whether it's a major issue like alcoholism or a less life-threatening issue like checking in with one another regularly about the relationship. Begin addressing the matter today, as this shows your partner that you don't take the relationship for granted. Unless you have unaddressed resentment toward your partner or you're seeking revenge on them, why would you want them to live with the difficulty of your issue even one more day? And if there is resentment, address that immediately, too. Don't let it simmer. Call the counselor, go to the meeting, get support.

~

A partnership is two people building a life together. Treat yours as such. Building a happy life together means bringing who you are—feelings, desires, challenges, dreams and all—and finding ways to mutually support one another in growing, healing, working through challenges, and being happy. If you're ruling over your partner or you're taking a backseat to your partner, that's not a partnership. A healthy partnership requires bravery because it takes both of you bringing all of who you are and working out how to best be together. Sometimes, the best version of your relationship means accepting the other in their flaws or unresolved issues. In other cases, the best version of the relationship means seeking self-transformation for the good of yourself, your partner, and the relationship. Many people complain that their partner doesn't accept them. Okay, that's fair, as acceptance plays a major role in maintaining relationships. On the other side of that issue, don't forget to ask yourself if there are areas of change you've been putting off. If you know something needs to change and it would be for the better, be cautious about complaining that your partner doesn't accept you. Maybe it's not a matter of acceptance; maybe it's a matter of them wanting a stronger connection with you. For example, to accept your partner not expressing how they feel is to also accept having a weak connection. It isn't necessarily that they're not accepting *you*, they're not accepting the *weak connection* that happens when you don't express your feelings. You might take it as criticism toward you, but from your partner's perspective, they want a strong relational connection with you. It's a high compliment to you that they want a stronger connection with you and that they won't accept a weak connection. Additionally, sometimes a lack of acceptance is the only thing that keeps a couple together. Going back to the example of alcoholism, if your partner accepts this is who you are and there's no chance of change, they might choose to leave. However, if they don't accept your drinking, they might stay in the relationship and fight for change. At some point, when change doesn't happen, most people will either leave the relationship in a literal sense or leave by withdrawing and no longer seeking connection. With this in mind, if there's an area you know needs to be worked on and changed, but you haven't yet addressed it, it's not necessarily bad that your partner doesn't accept you in this area. It means they still have hope for a better relationship together.

Partnerships aren't easy. It's difficult to navigate what's a matter of one partner being too picky and what's a matter of one partner not following through on changes necessary for the health of the relationship. But don't put it off if you've identified an area in the relationship that needs change.

Relationship Skill #13
Be Playful and Have Fun

Instead of being constantly serious, develop your fun, playful side.

For kids, everything can be play. A bed is a boat out on the sea. A piece of bread is bitten off into the shape of a gun. A weathered, old cement pad outside is a wedding aisle. It's fun to simply run, make noises, and look at tree branches on the ground.

In adulthood, a level of seriousness is required to get by. Applying for jobs or starting a business requires seriousness. The same applies to caring for children and driving a car. Most teenagers show up to plans if they want to. If they don't want to, they simply won't show up. There's no courtesy call and no consideration as to how the other person will feel. As an adult, not keeping your appointments results in lost opportunities, being viewed as untrustworthy, and no-show fees. It takes a certain amount of seriousness to use a scheduler, whether a device or physical planner.

Seriousness is important because it helps you focus so you can build and maintain a life as an adult. But does seriousness have a point of diminishing return? I think it does.

Seriousness serves one purpose: It helps you get things done. This is as true in partnerships as it is for life in general. A level of seriousness is required to find a therapist and schedule an appointment. There's also a level of seriousness required to act on addressing a dynamic within yourself that's negatively affecting your relationship. It takes seriousness to say to your partner, "Something's been weighing on my mind. I want to sit down and talk about it." A serious attitude aids in keeping your partnership on track.

The question here isn't whether you're a serious person or a happy-go-lucky person. Seriousness is required for adult relationships to thrive. The question is this: Can you transition back and forth from a serious attitude to a fun and playful attitude?

In adulthood, many people forget about their ability to have fun and be playful. For most of us, we were overwhelmed by what has been required of us in adulthood or have been hurt one too many times by people and organizations we trusted. Because of this, you may have decided to trust only yourself, thus experiencing the immense burden of doing life all alone, never seeking support. Being in "serious mode" most of the time will weigh on your partnership. Fun and play are the elements that balance out the weightiness of being serious. Without fun and play, your relationship can constantly seem like a heavy burden.

I was at a workshop where the participants had grown close to one another. During a break, I playfully jabbed a foam sword at a woman named Michelle. In response, she opened her arms as if to welcome the jabs, quite a spiritually serious response on par with turning the other cheek. After a moment, she said, "Wait, why did I do that?" She explained that she values a nonviolent attitude but that a playful jab from a foam sword is hardly violence. "You were just being playful," she said. Later in the workshop, I saw her playful side come out with a big smile on her face.

Play is not reserved for children 12 years of age and under. The issue is that skill is required to shift from the serious demands of life to a playful attitude. Take a moment and think about a few times when you had the most fun. Where were you, and what were you doing? Also, what was it about the environment you were in that you were comfortable enough to let go and be playful?

Between you and your partner, you'll both have to agree to let go and be playful occasionally. If one of you is always serious, play will not be that fun for the other.

Remember that play is not serious—*it's playful*. Some adults have difficulty distinguishing the difference because they've been so serious for so long. For example, growing up, my friend's father would chase us around the house and give us pink bellies. That means he'd hold us down and slap us repeatedly on the stomach. As a small child, it wasn't fun, it was terrifying. As another example, my much older cousin would hold me down and tickle me. I was only laughing because you can't help but laugh when being tickled. But it wasn't fun to be held down and tickled for an extended period. I wasn't happy to be around him. As another example, I was at a gathering where I didn't know most people, and a father played in the grass yard with his son, who looked about four years old. They would run around near one another, a lot like you might do in football, and then the father would forcefully push his son to the ground. It wasn't forceful enough to cause serious injuries, but enough that he wasn't gently going to the ground. It didn't look like much fun; it looked serious. I suspect people play with their kids in these ways because they want to teach their kids about life. You know, give your kids a hard time so they toughen up and learn about life. The logic makes sense, but you can teach kids about life through consequences and not through tossing them around or holding them down. All that teaches them is to not trust the people they're closest with. It requires a balance of instituting consequences and being kind and gentle to teach kids about life. They need to know that their actions have consequences, positive or negative, but they also need to learn to trust people and know that it's safe to be close to people and that gentle intimacy is available in the world. They need to learn to distinguish between safe people and dangerous people. But many of the "tough" lessons people impose on their children simply teach them there are *no* safe people at all. Parents teach their kids to trust only themselves and "go it alone" because that's how the parents live. If they knew supportive people were out there—and they are out there—I'm certain parents would want to guide their kids into learning how to connect with such people. Kids will experience difficulties in life, whether their parents were unnecessarily tough on them or gentle and kind to them. The only difference is that the kids whose parents were unnecessarily tough on them will have nobody to go to for support when life is hard, while the kids whose parents were gentle and kind will have a sense that support still exists even in the midst of difficulties. Kids with a sense of being unsupported become adults who think it's unsafe to be who they are. Ninety-nine percent of the relationship issues couples experience wouldn't exist if they both had a sense of being secure enough to be who they are and not what their defense mechanisms are. Many couples have an unconscious agreement to say nothing about the defense mechanisms of the other. This is categorized under acceptance of your partner, but in reality, it's mutually enabling one another not to have to peel away the defenses. There's always a sense that something isn't working, but neither person wants to say anything about it because it would also open them up to having their defense mechanisms pointed out (i.e., I won't point out your issues if you don't point out mine). Once again, this brings us to the question of if you'd rather face your honest challenges now or let them sit a while and later face the consequences of not having faced them.

Play requires dropping the defense mechanisms. Play will be unattainable if you won't drop the tough or macho persona. Play will be difficult if you won't come out of yourself and stop hiding and being hesitant. Play is kind and lighthearted.

Play could look like throwing a ball together. It could be going to Chuck E. Cheese together as adults, without children. My partner and I did this, and it was a blast. Play could mean tickling your partner for _one second_. Holding them down and tickling them for an extended time is not play, it's a form of torture. A playful comment might be, "I'm sorry, but you have to leave because your butt is too sexy, and it's distracting me," followed by walking over and smacking their butt. Saying, "Come here so I can smack your fat butt," is not play. That's unnecessarily demanding and an insult. Wrestling could be play but make it funnier and more sensual than a serious wrestling match.

Play is fun. If both people aren't having fun, it's not play for one of you. You'll have to examine which of two categories the issue is falling under: A) One of you is attempting to play, but it's coming off as insulting, mean, ugly, or invasive. B) One of you is being light-heartedly playful, but the other can't tap into their own playfulness. Before you blame your partner for a lack of fun and play in the relationship, consider whether your attempts at being playful fall into category A. If you are emulating category A, you'll need to be more kind, gentle, and light-hearted in your play and less hard-nosed. If you find you're emulating category

B, you'll have to access your silly side. Everything need not be about maintaining your image and keeping your defenses up in case someone comes at you. There are spontaneous, playful movements inside of you, and rigidity and withdrawal need to be set aside so they can come out.

Start small with play, especially if your partnership has been primarily serious. Go to the store together and get a bouncy ball or a glow-in-the-dark frisbee. If you've been in serious mode for a long time, too much play at once could be confusing or overwhelming. Practice introducing your system to transitioning back and forth from serious life tasks to fun and play.

Summary

We live in the world as adults. We were taught to get an education, build a career, have kids, and so on. But we weren't taught how to relate. Many of our ways of relating stem from automatic programming based on observations and interactions with the adults who raised us who also weren't taught how to relate. You then brought those same skills of relating into your partnership. Because of this, you need to learn to relate to your partner in healthy, adult ways instead of the conditioned ways you learned growing up.

Not seeking truth at all costs makes you vulnerable to maintaining habits that serve your ego but not the relationship. You satisfy the relationship and your deepest, truest self by seeking truth at all costs.

By sitting off in a corner and not using your voice, you rob yourself and your partner of the experience of relating with another human. A loving partner wants what's best for you. They want to hear your thoughts and opinions. While a loving partner may not do everything you want when you want (that's a servant, not a partner), they will be willing to continue the discussion until the two of you find a way forward that's mutually agreeable. The solution may not be perfect for either of you, but it will consider both your needs and desires. Give your partner the gift of mutually building a life together instead of going through life separately while under the same roof.

Whenever you bring up an issue or seek to make a change in the relationship, own the decision for yourself. Don't do it because your therapist told you to, do it because you believe in it. Consider if you like the idea even if it was your therapist's suggestion. If you do, own it for yourself. When you say things like, "My therapist told me to . . ." it can give your partner a sense that you're not thinking for yourself. Taking ownership of your decisions gives your partner a sense of building a life with you personally, not with your therapist through you.

Without putting in the effort to make up after harmful words and actions or lack of words and actions, your relationship can disintegrate quickly. Acting like it never happened won't cut it, nor will saying things like, "I'm sorry you feel that way." To come back into trust and a positive connection with you, your partner needs to know that you understand what you did was wrong and why it was hurtful. If you don't take responsibility for your hurtful actions, even if it means losing your self-image of always being a good and trustworthy person or always being right, you put your partner in a difficult position. They must choose between a) forcing themselves to remain in connection with you even though you haven't taken ownership or b) not coming back into connection. Neither is a pleasant choice. After hurtful events, make it easy for your partner to come back into trust and a positive connection.

Unlike child-parent or child-caregiver relationships, adult relationships aren't to be taken for granted. Be careful about wanting to fulfill the love you didn't receive from your parents through your partner. Children need unconditional love from their parents (note that unconditional love does not mean love without necessary discipline and consequences). Adult relationships require honesty and respect. Moving in together or even saying "I do" is not grounds for taking your relationship for granted. Don't agree to anything you can't follow through on. When you agree to something, follow through. That's how you build a life with your partner. If one or neither of you cannot be counted on to follow through on your agreed-upon ways of doing life together, then you won't be able to build a life together. You'll be living separate, frustrated lives under the same roof.

Circling back to unconditional love, your partner may meet your needs for love occasionally or even often. Don't take that as a signal to stop showing them that you can be trusted and relied upon. It's a partnership, not a you-do-what-I-want-but-I-don't-consider-you-and-your-feelings-ship—the latter is a childlike attitude. Partner up with your significant other and discuss how you can each show up for one another and meet one another's relational needs. Don't expect perfection from one another but do expect a reasonable effort. When you take your partner for granted, pause and reflect upon what brought you to that place. Were there times in your relationship you didn't take them for granted, like when you were first dating? What's happened in your personal life or partnership that has led you to take them for granted now?

When in conversation, remember to have a balance of sharing and listening, hearing and being heard between the two of you. Listening means putting aside your thoughts for the moment and taking in what your partner is saying. When you're uncertain about what your partner wants to get through to you, ask clarifying questions to get on the same page.

Do you ever feel similar ways in your relationship you felt growing up? You could be putting a projection of your past onto your partner. In an example earlier in the book, my client's wife projected onto him that he would be aggressive and unopen to her vulnerable feelings because he was an adult man living in the same home as her. This was a projection of her father onto

134

my client. Emotions and fears are never just imaginary. They exist, but it's a matter of determining whether the danger is outside of yourself or a projection of emotional pain still alive within you from past experiences. Maybe there is no external danger, just unresolved past emotional wounds and traumas.

Remember that providing a living isn't equivalent to a healthy, happy partnership. There must be a capacity to care about the things that matter to your partner and have your partner care about the things that matter to you. Additionally, without sharing who you are on the inside and receiving who your partner is on the inside, then both of you respecting what you see, you'll be hard-pressed to form a connection with one another. With that said, if your partner works hard, whether at a career or raising the kids and maintaining the home, don't let yourself forget to express appreciation.

Be cautious about continually talking about issues but not acting on them. Conversation feels good because you're discussing the things weighing on you. But without taking action to address the problems in your partnership, conversations can become meaningless. It still feels good to talk because it's like releasing a pressure valve. In addition, there might be that splinter of hope that your partner might hear you this time and take action so you continue having conversations. Don't just talk about the issues in your partnership; take the actions required to address them.

And finally, the one so many adults forget about: fun and play. Without these elements, a partnership can become like a field of planted seeds in a drought. If you think your relationship needs to be refreshed, fun and play could be the rain you need.

Moving forward, it can be helpful to keep one question in mind: Where are my words and actions coming from—are they a conscious decision based in the present or do they stem from old, conditioned ways of relating?

One Last Thing

If you haven't already, would you leave a review of this book on Amazon? Your review is a great way to help others understand how they can benefit from this book. On the book's product page, find the button that reads "Write a review" or "Write a customer review". From there, one or two sentences about what you got out of this book would be more than enough.

Workbook

The workbook companion to *Adult Relationship Skills* is available on Amazon.

Get in Touch

I like hearing from readers.

You can send me an email at **nic@nicsaluppo.com**.

More from this Author

Communicate Your Feelings (without starting a fight)
What to Say and What Not to Say to Your Partner

Learn to communicate effectively so you and your partner can have productive conversations about difficult topics. Read the full book description and get a sample on Amazon.

Learn to Love Yourself Again
A Step-by-Step Guide to Conquer Self-Hatred, Ditch Self-Loathing, & Cultivate Self-Compassion

In American society, we tend to equate self love with accomplishments and being better than others at something, resulting in endless efforts to do and be more, all to the point of exhaustion. Also, what are we supposed to do when there's something about ourselves we really dislike (or outright hate)? Get off the hamster wheel and learn true self love. Read the full book description and get a sample on Amazon.

Outsmart Negative Thinking
Simple Mindfulness Methods to Control Negative Thoughts, Stop Anxiety, & Finally Experience Happiness

Stop letting your anxious brain and ceaseless negative thought cycles hold you back. Read the full book description and get a sample on Amazon.

Made in United States
North Haven, CT
12 May 2024

52436642R00083